Scholastic Guides

SUPER STUDY SKILLS

THE ULTIMATE GUIDE TO TESTS AND STUDYING

Laurie Rozakis, Ph.D.

SCHOLASTIC REFERENCE

To Mary Varilla Jones: Mary, A good editor is a priceless treasure —
and you're one of the best. Your intelligence, kindness, and true
professionalism have made writing this book an absolute pleasure.
In grateful appreciation, I dedicate this book to you.

Library of Congress Cataloging-in-Publication Data
Rozakis, Laurie.
Super study skills / Laurie Rozakis.
p. cm. — (Scholastic guides)
Includes index.
1. Study skills—Juvenile literature. 2. Test-taking skills—Juvenile literature. 3. Exam-
inations—Juvenile literature. [1. Study skills. 2. Test-taking skills.] I. Title. II. Series.

LB1049 .R68 2002
3713.3'028'1—dc21   2001020032

· 0-439-21601-X (POB)
0-439-21607-9 (PB)

Book design by Kay Petronio

10 9 8 7 6 5 4 3 2 1   02 03 04 05 06

Printed in the U.S.A.   23
First printing, August 2002

Curriculum Consultants: Bob Stremme, Daniela Silvestri

CONTENTS

INTRODUCTION

Is studying a chore? Do you forget material you just read? Does test taking give you a sick feeling in the pit of your stomach? Schoolwork doesn't have to be something you dread. You can make studying and test taking easier. You **can** be a super student — it's not that hard! Start with this math:

SUBJECT SKILLS + SMART STUDY = SCHOOL SUCCESS

Scholastic's *Super Study Skills* can make it happen. In this book, you'll learn how to . . .

- make the most of your time by getting organized.
- read more effectively.
- prepare for a test without last-minute panic.
- take tests with confidence and skill.
- study smarter to get the grades you want.

Here's what you'll learn in each part of this book:

Section One: Study Smart! shows you how to set realistic goals and make the most of your study time. You'll learn how to improve your memory and take great notes, too.

Section Two: Read for Success teaches you how to take charge of your reading by previewing, predicting, and setting a purpose. You'll also discover easy ways to get the most from a text.

Section Three: Preparing for a Test shows you how to make the most of your pre-test study time. Should you study alone or in a group?

Should you cram? The answers are in this section, along with ways to calm test jitters.

Section Four: Test-Taking Skills takes you step-by-step through the actual testing situation. Before, during, and after the test: It's all here! There's even a section on evaluating your performance to help you do better next time.

Section Five: Mastering Specific Tests provides short-answer test hints and essay test hints, so you'll be prepared for any test you take.

Scholastic's *Super Study Skills* makes it possible for you to do your very best in school. Let your talent shine through!

STUDY SMART!

Studying brings short-term and long-term rewards. Right now, good study habits help you learn more in school and remember it better. Your self-confidence will soar as people praise your achievements. Studying smarter also leaves you more time for sports and clubs. Later on, those same good study habits will help you do well in your job. You'll find it easier to make smart life choices, too. Start by getting the right attitude.

YOU CAN SUCCEED!

Have you ever felt this way?

> "I'm just not smart enough to learn all this stuff."
> "My friends won't like me if I get A's on tests."
> "The teacher isn't good, so I'll never be able to learn."

If you talk yourself into failing, you probably will fail. But if you talk yourself into success, you have a good chance of doing well. Study smart by having a positive attitude about school and yourself.

Start by . . .

- being enthusiastic about learning.
- having discipline.
- deciding that you can do well on tests.
- having self-respect.
- making friends with people who support your hopes and dreams.
- not being a quitter.
- preparing for the future.
- using your time wisely.

Be a Class Act

"The teacher doesn't like me," you say. Actually, you may be right. Teachers are human, like you. They tend to judge students by the way they act. When you treat your teachers with respect, they will treat you with respect. If you do your work to the best of your ability and take school seriously, your teacher will respond. Get with the program by taking an active and positive role in the classroom.

- Be prepared. Bring your books, notebooks, homework, pencils, pens, and erasers.
- Sit in the front of the room. This reduces distractions and shows the teacher that you are serious about learning.
- Pay close attention in class.
- Take good notes.

- Raise your hand when you know the answer.
- Ask intelligent questions when you're confused.
- Resist peer pressure to misbehave.
- Treat your teachers with courtesy.
- Come to every class.

Goal Oriented

What do you want to be when you grow up? You might know what you want to be. Perhaps you have a general idea of a job. Maybe you don't have any plans for the future.

Setting goals can help you study more effectively. You can set *short-term goals* and *long-term goals*. Short-term goals look ahead an hour, day, week, or months. Long-term goals are set years in the future.

Good students set short-term goals and long-term goals. Often, the two types of goals work together. For example, if you set a goal to learn three new words a week, you'll do better in class. This helps you earn higher grades, which helps your long-term goal of attending college come true.

Make a timeline to show your goals and the steps you'll follow. Here's a sample:

GOAL: To raise my grades by the next marking period.

	January	*February*	*March*
Week 1	Write down all assignments.	Attend extra help.	Check my progress.
Week 2	No TV until homework is done.	Cut computer cybersurfing.	No music while studying.
Week 3	Take better notes.	Get a study buddy.	Visit the library weekly.
Week 4	Reread notes every night before bed.	Read one extra book a week.	Reward myself!

SEIZE THE DAY

Michael comes home from school every day and feeds his cat. He plays some video games, has a snack, and reads his e-mail. By then it's time for dinner. After dinner, Michael reads the comics and does some chores. Suddenly, it's time for bed — but Michael has not even started his homework. His parents are furious and his brother is laughing at him. Michael can't figure out where all his time went.

Time has a sneaky way of slipping away. Fortunately, you can get control of your time by making a study schedule. A study schedule helps you set goals as well as get your work done. A study schedule also helps you . . .

- break down the task into manageable parts.
- keep up with assignments.
- get into a study routine.
- make the most of your time.

Here's the study schedule Michael made:

TIME	MON.	TUES.	WED.	THURS.	FRI.	WEEK-END
3:00 PM	snack/ play	music lesson	snack/ play	religious education	snack/ play	snack/ play
4:00 PM	homework	homework	homework	homework	homework	study
5:00 PM	dinner	dinner	dinner	dinner	dinner	dinner
6:00 PM	soccer practice	chores	chores	soccer practice	chores	chores
7:00 PM	reading	reading	reading	reading	reading	reading
8:00 PM	study	study	study	study	study	study
9:00 PM	prepare for the next day (pack backpack and lunch, set out clothes)					

By setting aside blocks of time for homework and study, this schedule leaves Michael plenty of time to unwind after school. Notice that he gets his homework done *before* dinner so he has time *after* dinner to read, study, and still have time for other activities. There's also some extra time built in at the end of the evening in case Michael has a big test or a lot of reading one night.

Michael gets ready for school the night before to avoid early morning panic. Michael penciled in some study time on weekends so he'll be all set for school on Monday.

Make a Study Schedule

Use the following blank form for your study schedule. Fix the schedule to fit your individual needs. For example, you might want to study in the morning *before* school as well as in the afternoon and evening *after* school. Make photocopies of the schedule and post them in your room to help you become the master of your fate. Don't force your parents to become "Homework Police"!

TIME	MON.	TUES.	WED.	THURS.	FRI.	SAT.	SUN.
7:00 AM							
8:00 AM							
3:00 PM							
4:00 PM							
5:00 PM							
6:00 PM							
7:00 PM							
8:00 PM							
9:00 PM							

It's not enough to make a study schedule; you also have to follow it!

GET ORGANIZED

Nicole raced into class, five minutes late as usual. "Where's your homework, Nicole?" the teacher asked with a sigh.

"This time I really did it, Ms. Taylor," Nicole said as she rummaged through her backpack. "But . . . uh . . . I seem to have forgotten it," she muttered.

"Along with your textbook and pen — again?" Ms. Taylor said with a frown.

Poor Nicole! She keeps forgetting things. That's because she's not organized.

Organization is one of the keys to effective studying and test taking. In fact, organization can help you succeed in every part of your life.

The following page contains a checklist of materials you will need in school and for homework. Photocopy the list and use it to check off your supplies each day. Then you won't forget anything important.

HOME SUPPLIES

_____ assignment pad

_____ binders or notebooks

_____ calculator

_____ dictionary

_____ paper

_____ pens

_____ pencils

_____ pencil sharpener

_____ ruler

_____ school books

_____ telephone numbers and
e-mail addresses of
homework buddies

_____ watch or clock

SCHOOL SUPPLIES

_____ assignment pad

_____ binders or notebooks

_____ calculator

_____ dictionary

_____ gym clothes

_____ homework (completed)

_____ paper

_____ pens

_____ pencils

_____ school books

_____ watch or clock

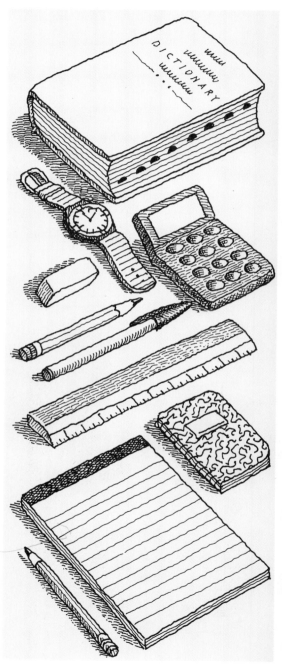

> **T I P**
> **Pack all your school supplies the night before and put your backpack by the door. Grab your backpack as you leave and you'll be all set for school success!**

SET UP A STUDY CENTER

Make the most of your study time by setting up a study center. A study center helps you concentrate on your work and get into the habit of studying. The following chart shows you which places work well — and which ones don't!

GREAT STUDY AREAS	POOR STUDY AREAS
in your room at a desk	in front of the television
in a calm corner of the house	in your room on the bed
in a quiet part of the school or public library	on the school bus

Your study center should have good light, your study tools (textbooks, reference books, paper, pens), and quiet. You can't study if music is blaring, if you're talking to friends, or if Fido is barking to be let out.

- Study in a calm, quiet place.
- Turn off the television, radio, and other distractions.
- Study at the same time each day so people know to leave you alone.

A Note on Computers

If you're lucky enough to have your own computer, it should be a central part of your study center. Computers can help you prepare well-organized notes, make easy-to-read outlines, and write essays and reports.

If your family has a computer in another part of the house, set up a quiet time to use it for homework and studying. Find a time that is convenient for you and everyone else, too. For example, if the computer is in the family room, you might want to use it at 3:00 in the afternoon, when your family members are in another part of the house. You wouldn't want to use it from 8:00 to 10:00 at night, when everyone else is watching television in the same room.

Make an "appointment" to use the computer at the same time every day. Your family members will know that you're serious about working on the computer and will respect your determination.

GET A STUDY BUDDY

Try the buddy system — the *study* buddy system, that is! Find a buddy in each class and trade telephone numbers. You can call your study buddy to get assignments you forgot to write down or missed because you were absent. You can contact your study buddy to talk about assignments you don't understand, too. Finally, you can review material for tests with your study buddy.

How can you select good study buddies? Look for classmates who . . .

- take school seriously.
- earn higher grades than you do right now.
- keep up with all the work.
- are trustworthy.
- are well-organized.
- are rarely — if ever — absent.

Even if the study buddy you select is in all your classes, select at least three study buddies so you always have a backup person to contact. You might also want to find at least one study buddy with e-mail.

Be sure to have at least three homework buddies, friends you can call for help with assignments.

IMPROVE YOUR MEMORY

Tests show how much you remember and understand. Try these ideas for beefing up your memory.

1. **Link it**

    Connect new ideas to what you already know. For example, if you know that *either* is spelled *ei* rather than *ie*, you can use this to learn that *neither* is spelled with the same pattern.

2. **Repeat it**

    Repetition helps fix information in your mind, so recite facts aloud or write them down. You might have used this technique by writing spelling words over and over to help memorize them. Try it now with these tricky spelling words: *chocolate, laboratory, February, spaghetti, forty.*

3. **Play with it**

    Use memory tricks, little sayings that jog your mind. For example, if you want to remember the order of the planets, try learning this saying: *My Very Educated Mother Just Served Us Nine Pizzas.* The first letter of each word shows the order of the planets: Mercury, Venus, Earth, Mars, Jupiter, Saturn, Uranus, Neptune, Pluto.

You can use well-known memory tricks like these examples or create your own.

Here are a few more familiar memory tricks:

SUBJECT AREA	MEMORY TRICK	STANDS FOR
Spelling	*i* before *e*, except after *c* or as sounded as *a* as in *neighbor* and *weigh*	spelling *ie/ei* words
Music	Every good boy does fine	E,G,B,D,F lines in clef
Music	FACE	F,A,C,E spaces in clef
Math	Please excuse my dear aunt Sally	parentheses, exponents, multiplication, division, addition, subtraction

4. **Write it down**

   Write important information on index cards. Use these flash cards often to help you remember historic dates, definitions, vocabulary, math formulas, and other facts and ideas.

5. **Sing it**

   Songs stick in our mind because of their strong rhythm. Set important facts such as state capitals, presidents, and science facts to songs to help fix them in your mind.

6. **Visualize it**

   As you study, form a mental picture of a person, place, thing, or idea. Do this by imagining how it looks, smells, sounds, tastes, or feels.

TAKE GREAT NOTES

Taking super notes reinforces what you learn as well as helps you remember what you hear. Good notes also serve as a study guide that helps you get top grades on tests. Here's how to take great notes:

1. **Write only the important information**

   When you are listening in class or reading at home, write down the main points. These include . . .

   • the main idea.

   • important names, dates, numbers.

   • key details.

   • any questions you have about the material.

   To find the key information, listen or read for word clues, such as *the most important reason, the main point,* or *this will be on the test.* Teachers and writers often repeat vital facts in different ways, so watch for repetition. Pay special attention at the very beginning or end of a lecture, when a teacher often introduces and summarizes the main points. The same is true in a reading.

2. Outline and highlight

When you are taking notes from a textbook, arrange your notes in an outline. Follow the book's organization. Then go back over your outline and highlight the most important information. You can also highlight the key facts in any notes you take in class.

Here's an example of a lecture on the skeleton:

As babies we start off with about 300 bones in our skeleton, but some bones join together as we grow. There are 206 separate bones in an adult's body.

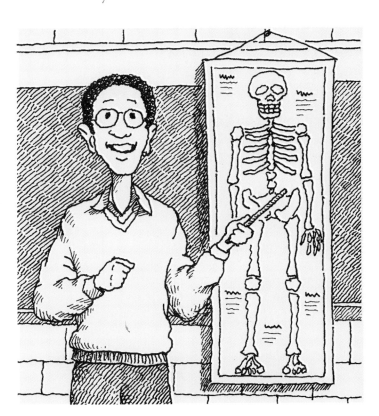

Have you ever wondered why we need a skeleton? One important reason concerns our muscles and internal organs. They are very soft and need protection. Some organs need more protection than others. For instance, our brain and spinal cord are protected by the skull and spine. The heart, liver, lungs, and intestines are all easily damaged, so they are protected by our ribs, hip bones, and spine.

Skeletons also help us stand up. Without a skeleton, we would slump into a heap. Our muscles are strong, but without a skeleton we wouldn't have anything to pull against and we would be unable to stand up or move.

After hearing this lecture, your notes might look like this:

I. Skeleton 300 bones in child, 206 bones in adult
    because bones fuse.
    a. enables us to stand and move
    b. protects muscles and internal organs
        1. skull and spine protect brain and spinal cord
        2. ribs, hip bones, and spine protect heart, liver,
           lungs, intestines

How many muscles do we have?

These notes include several main points and are in outline form. They also include a question about the material:

I. Skeleton 300 bones in child, 206 bones in adult	*important*
because bones fuse	*numbers*
a. enables us to stand and move	*main idea*
b. protects muscles and internal organs	
1. skull and spine protect brain and spinal cord	*key detail*
2. ribs, hip bones, and spine protect heart, liver,	
lungs, intestines	
How many muscles do we have?	*question*

3. **Keep it brief!**

   To help you keep up with a lecture, develop a system of abbreviations. For example:

$$+ \text{ or } \& \quad = \quad \text{and}$$
$$\text{b/c} \quad = \quad \text{because}$$
$$\text{w/} \quad = \quad \text{with}$$

Here's how to make the notes you read before easier to write:

I. Skeleton 300 bones in child, 206 bones in adult
       b/c bones fuse
           a. enables us to stand + move
           b. protects muscles + internal organs
               1. skull and spine protect brain and spinal cord
               2. ribs, hip bones, and spine protect heart, liver,
                  lungs, intestines

How many muscles do we have?

You can also use sketches, charts, and lists to separate the important facts from the minor details.

4. **Organize your notes**

    Keep your notes in a binder, organized by topic. Also keep any handouts the teacher gives you in your binder. When you study, you'll have all your notes in one place.

5. **Write clearly**

    Your notes will be useless unless you can read them! If you take messy notes, rewrite them soon after class when your memory is fresh.

TIP

Always copy down everything a teacher writes on the board. If it's on the board, you can assume it's important. Be careful to copy the words the way the teacher spelled them.

READ FOR SUCCESS

It's no secret that being a good reader makes every part of your schoolwork easier — especially studying and taking tests. Happily, reading doesn't have to be a chore. In this part of the book, you'll learn many ways to make reading easier and more fun. Try each of the methods and decide which ones work best for you. You can also use different techniques when you read fiction (stories and novels) and nonfiction (textbooks, essays, articles).

How can you get the most from the reading techniques that you will learn in this part of the book? Start by trying these three ideas:

1. Be an Explorer

- Try each reading method several times with different types of texts, such as stories, textbooks, Web pages, and newspaper articles.

- You will probably find one or two reading methods that you like a lot. Stick with them, but try new ones, too. Don't get stuck in a reading rut!

2. Practice Makes Perfect

- Practice these reading techniques 15 to 20 minutes a day. Follow the schedule, and you'll see progress fast.

- Try reading at the same time every day, in the same place, so you get into a reading routine.

3. Stick with It

- Keep a "reading diary" by listing all the different things you have read. You'll feel good looking back at all the fun you've had reading.

- Don't give up! Learning any skill takes time and effort, but it's really worth it.

Below are the techniques that will help you improve your reading skills. Use these methods as you study, take tests, and read for pleasure. Every one of these reading methods will help you in all the reading you do.

BE AN ACTIVE READER

When you meet a new person for the first time, you don't say, "Entertain me." Instead, you share your experiences, your ideas, and your dreams as you listen to the other person's thoughts. In the process, you often learn as much about yourself as you do about your new friend.

You can create the same exciting relationship with a writer when you read a new book. Don't wait for the book to entertain you; instead, get to know the book by becoming an *active reader*!

Use the following techniques to become an active reader.

Preview the Text

Before you read or study, preview the text by taking a "sneak peek." First see if you're reading *fiction* (a made-up story) or *nonfiction* (a real-life account of a person, place, thing, or idea). You'll probably read fiction quickly because you'll be swept along with the plot, characters, and setting. You'll probably read nonfiction more slowly because you'll be concentrating on the ideas. You will reread important and difficult parts of the text, too.

Then *preview* the reading by examining the different parts of the text. Active readers — like you! — preview a text to help them know what they will discover as they read.

Preview these parts of *this* book:

• the cover	Look at the words and art.
• the title	*Super Study Skills: The Ultimate Guide to Tests and Studying.*
• the table of contents and subtitles	See pages 3–6.
• pictures, illustrations, photographs, charts, or maps	Flip through the book.
• the captions	See how the art is described.

> **T**
> **I**
> **P**
>
> **You can often define an unfamiliar word by taking it apart and finding the little words it contains. For example, you can tell that the word *preview* means to "look before" from its prefix *pre* (before) and root *view* (look). Make it a habit to review all *affixes* — the prefixes and suffixes.**

Preview the Cover

Bet you've heard the old saying, "You can't judge a book by its cover." Actually, you *can*! Previewing a book by looking at its cover can tell you a lot about what's inside. Before you start to read a book, examine its front and back covers.

As you study the covers, ask yourself these questions:

- What clues about the story do I get from the title? Based on the title, what do I think will happen in the story?

- What clues about the story do I get from the pictures on the front and back covers? For example, will this book be happy, sad, scary, or informative?

- Who wrote the book? Have I read any other books by this author?

- Did any famous people comment about the book on the back cover? If so, what do their comments tell me about the book?

- Inside the jacket flaps, if any, how is the story described?

Preview the Title

Now read the book's title. See what it tells you about the contents. For example, you can ask yourself the following questions if you're reading a novel:

- What does the title mean? Does it have more than one meaning?

- What reasons could the writer have for choosing this title?

- Based on the title, what do I predict will happen in the story?

Preview the Table of Contents and Subtitles

Open the book and scan the table of contents. If you're reading an article or chapter, flip the pages, read the subtitles, and ask questions. For example, if you're reading a nonfiction book such as this one, you could ask yourself these questions:

- What will this book teach me?
- What main topics does this book cover?
- How are the topics arranged? What will I read first, second, and so on?

Preview Any Pictures, Illustrations, Photographs, Charts, or Maps

One picture may be worth a thousand words, especially when it comes to previewing and making predictions! When you look at the pictures, ask yourself these questions:

- What different types of pictures, photographs, and maps are included?
- What do each of these visuals show?
- What mood or tone do they convey? For example, does this look like a cheerful story or a mysterious story?
- Why did the writer include these illustrations? What purpose do they serve?
- Based on the pictures, what do I think this reading will be about?

Preview the Captions

Most pictures, photographs, and other illustrations have captions. These sentences, usually placed under the pictures, may describe what is shown in the pictures or add additional information. As you preview the captions, ask yourself:

- What facts do I get from the captions?
- Based on the captions, what does this book describe?

MAKE PREDICTIONS

After you preview the text, it's time to make predictions about its contents. When you *make predictions*, you make educated guesses about what's to come. The process looks like this:

WHAT I KNOW + STORY CLUES = PREDICTION

As you read, your brain is always trying to figure out what's coming next in the story. As a result, you make predictions *before* you read and *while* you read. Once you find out what's coming next, you confirm or change your predictions. If you're reading a novel or story, you ask yourself:

- "Based on what I know and clues in the story, what do I think will happen next?"
- "How accurate were my predictions?"
- "What new predictions can I make using the facts I just read?"

For example, if you previewed a passage called "Leaders of the Pack," you might predict that the story would be about presidents, kings, or even dogs! As you read on, you confirm your guess to see if you were or were not on target. You stay one step ahead by making predictions.

Prediction Place

Now stop and think about what you've learned from previewing the text and making predictions. If you're a little confused, go back to the text and look again. See what additional information you can get to help you figure out what you will learn from this reading. Then state your predictions in a sentence. Here are some models:

I predict that this book will describe_____.

I predict that the main character will_____.

I predict that I will learn that _____.

I predict that I will like this book because _____.

Try it with the following reading about the Supreme Court. Follow these steps:

1. Preview the passage.

2. Make predictions.

3. Read the passage to confirm or change your predictions.

Write your answers on a separate sheet of paper.

The Supreme Court: The Highest Court in the Land

America's federal system of courts is like a pyramid, with state courts on the bottom and federal courts in the middle. At the very top of

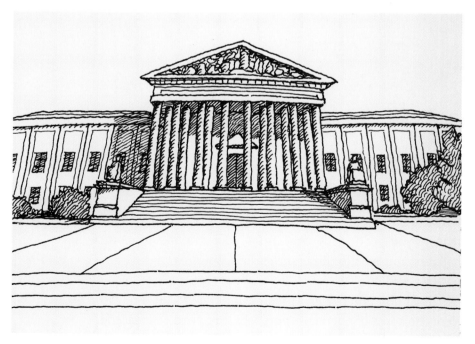

The Supreme Court held its first session on February 2, 1790.

the pyramid is the Supreme Court, the "court of last resort." The nine Supreme Court justices have "original jurisdiction" (the power to try cases that have not been previously tried by a lower court) over very few types of cases. They may try problems between two states, for example, or a case involving an ambassador. However, these cases are rare. Instead, most of the Supreme Court's time is spent reviewing decisions that have already been made in lower courts. Each year, the Supreme Court justices receive more than 5,000 cases to review. They accept only the most important ones. The Supreme Court considers cases that demand a decision about the meaning of the Constitution or a federal law. When the Supreme Court reaches a decision about a case, it is final. Its decisions result in laws that affect us all.

SET A PURPOSE FOR READING

Why are you reading this book? Are you reading this book for the same reason you read an e-mail from your friend? Of course not! That's because you read for different reasons. Your reason for reading is your *purpose* for reading.

After you preview and predict, it's time to set a purpose for reading. Here are some of the main purposes you have for reading:

- To confirm a belief

- To discover opinions
- To get facts
- To get instructions
- To have fun
- To learn new information
- To learn new vocabulary
- To review notes

Your Purpose for Reading Shapes the Way You Read

When you study, you read slowly so you understand and remember the material. You don't want to miss any facts or details that could be important. You also take notes to record key words, dates, and facts. If you own the book or are reading a paper you can keep, you can highlight important material. If you are reading to be entertained, however, you read more quickly. You might even skim some of the descriptions in your haste to see how the story turns out!

Setting a Purpose Saves Time

If you know why you're reading, you can go straight to the book or article that has the information you need. You won't waste time reading material that you don't need at that time.

Setting a Purpose Improves Understanding

By setting a purpose for reading, you'll be sure to get the most out of what you read. Knowing what you want to find out helps you concentrate on that information and remember it better, too.

Below are two different readings. Preview each one, make predictions, and set a purpose for reading. Then read each selection. See how previewing, predicting, and setting a purpose for reading helped you get more from the passage.

Reading #1

Build Your Own Terrarium

Place two handfuls of small pebbles in the bottom of a clear, widemouthed plastic jar. On top of the pebbles, add two handfuls of soil. Then arrange a handful of mulch (dead leaves) on top of the soil. Using a pencil or tongs, gently poke holes in the soil layers. In the

A terrarium is a clear container filled with living things, air, soil, and water.

holes, plant several small plants or ferns in a pretty arrangement. Tap the soil down gently. Fill in around the plants with moss. When the planting is complete, water the terrarium with a squeeze bottle, or sprinkle water lightly over the entire inside of the jar. Be careful not to overwater the terrarium, or the plants could become moldy. Place the lid on the jar. Since your miniworld has everything it needs to survive, you can keep the lid closed. Place the jar in indirect light.

Reading #2

Baby in the Crib

John stole a pig from Old Henry. John was on his way home with the pig when Old Henry saw him. After John got home, he up and saw Old Henry coming down to the house. So John put the pig in a cradle they used to rock babies in those days (some people called them cribs), and covered the pig all up. When Old Henry walked in, John was sitting there rocking the crib.

Old Henry said, "What's the matter with the baby, John?"

"The baby's got the measles," John answered. Suspecting that John was trying to

What's a pig doing in a baby's cradle?

trick him, Old Henry demanded, "I want to see him." John replied, "Well, you can't; the doctor said if you uncover him the measles will go back in him and kill him."

So Old Henry got angrier and angrier and shouted, "I don't care; I want to see him, John." He reached down to uncover him.

John said, "If that baby is turned to a pig now, don't blame me."

Based on your preview, you probably read "Build Your Own Terrarium" to find out how you could make your own indoor garden under glass. The picture of the terrarium and the caption suggested that this reading would give instructions.

However, you probably read "Baby in the Crib" for enjoyment. The cute picture of a pig in a cradle suggested that this story would be fun to read. The caption might also have sparked your interest in solving the mystery: What *is* a pig doing in a baby's cradle?

USE WHAT YOU KNOW

You know a lot more than you think! You can use what you know to make your reading easier and more fun. Connecting new facts with your prior knowledge helps you remember new information when you study it.

After you preview, predict, and set a purpose for reading, take a few minutes to jot down notes about what you already know about the passage. Ask yourself, "What do I know about this subject?" Decide what you want to find out, too. After you finish reading, you can complete your chart by writing down what you learned.

You can arrange your ideas on a chart like this one:

WHAT I KNOW	WHAT I WANT TO FIND OUT	WHAT I LEARNED

Read the following passage. On a separate piece of paper, fill out the chart.

The Statue of Liberty

Given by the people of France to the people of the United States as a symbol of a shared love of freedom and everlasting friendship, the Statue of Liberty is one of the largest freestanding statues ever created. It weighs 450,000 pounds and rises 151 feet above its pedestal. More than 100 feet around, Ms. Liberty has eyes two and a half feet wide, a mouth three feet wide, and a nose four and a half feet long. Her upraised right arm stretches forty-two feet; her hand is nearly seventeen feet long. Her fingers are close to ten feet long. About thirty people can stand in the head at the same time. Twelve people can fit in the torch. The statue has an iron framework that keeps it from toppling over. People around the world recognize the Statue of Liberty.

The Statue of Liberty stands on Liberty Island at the
entrance to New York Harbor.

Here's how Lourdes filled out the chart, based on her preview and purpose for reading:

WHAT I KNOW	WHAT I WANT TO FIND OUT	WHAT I LEARNED
The Statue of Liberty is one of the largest statues ever built.	How big the Statue of Liberty really is.	It weighs 450,000 pounds.
		It rises 151 feet.
		It is over 100 feet around.
		The eyes are 2 1/2 feet wide.
		The mouth is 3 feet wide.
		The nose is 4 1/2 feet long.
		The arm is 42 feet long.
		The hand is 17 feet long.
		The fingers are 10 feet long.
		30 people fit in the head
		12 people fit in the torch.
		It has an iron frame.

SKIM THE TEXT

When you want to get a general idea about a text, you skim it. *Skimming* is a very fast method of reading that lets you glance at a passage to get its main idea or to find a key point.

Skimming makes reading easier because it helps you focus on the important parts of the text. When you go back and read the text in detail, you can zero in on the parts you have to study. You won't spend time lost in detail.

Follow these steps as you skim a reading:

1. Preview the text by looking at the title, subheadings, pictures, and captions.

2. Make predictions and set a purpose for reading.

3. Start skimming by running your eyes across the page. Try to read as fast as you can.

4. Focus on the key words. These will be nouns and verbs.

5. Look for the facts you need. These will often be in the first and last sentences. Read these facts more slowly.

6. Pause at the end of every page or passage to restate the meaning in your own words. If you are alone, you can say the words aloud. If you are in class, say the words silently.

TIP

Skimming isn't a substitute for a complete reading. Skim *before* you read the text . . . not *instead* of reading it.

Skim the following passage to get a general idea of its meaning.

A Night to Remember

Just before midnight on April 14, 1912, one of the most famous ocean disasters occurred, the sinking of the *Titanic*. The *Titanic* was the fanciest ship at the time, with its beautiful rooms, glittering crystal chandeliers, and delicious food. In addition, it was supposed to be the safest ocean liner ever built. The hull was divided into sixteen supposedly watertight compartments. According to the ship's manufacturer, four of the sixteen compartments could be flooded without threatening the ship's ability to float. That April, the majestic ocean liner was on its first voyage, traveling from Southampton, England, to New York City. On the evening of April 14, the ship was sailing 95 miles south of Newfoundland when it collided with a gigantic iceberg. The ship sank because the iceberg tore five of the sixteen watertight compartments. The "unsinkable" *Titanic* vanished under the water at 2:20 A.M., April 15. There were about 2,200 passengers aboard, and all but 678 died. The tragedy was made even worse by the crew's useless rescue attempts. Since there weren't enough lifeboats, the crew's efforts to save people failed.

Here's one way to state the general idea: "The *Titanic* sunk when it hit an iceberg. Many people died."

FIND THE MAIN IDEA

"What's your point?" When was the last time you said this to a friend? When you try to find out the most important point a friend is making, you are looking for the *main idea*. A main idea is the most important point that a speaker or writer is making. The main idea tells what the whole passage is about.

Every *detail,* or small piece of information in the passage, gives information to support or explain the main idea. When you find the main idea, you know the author's point. This helps you understand the whole passage more clearly. In some cases, the main idea will be directly stated in a passage. In other cases, you will have to figure out the main idea from clues in the passage.

> **TIP**
>
> **The stated main idea in a paragraph is also called the *topic sentence*.**

Find a Stated Main Idea

To find the stated main idea in a paragraph, follow these steps:

1. Find the topic or subject of the paragraph.

2. Look for a sentence that tells about the topic. It will explain what the entire paragraph is about.

3. Check to see if the sentence tells what the paragraph is about.

   Although the stated main idea is often the first sentence, it can be in the middle or end of a paragraph as well. Below are some examples. The main idea is underlined in each one.

Main idea in the *beginning* of a paragraph:

The Florida landscape boasts a wide variety of plant life — about 3,500 different kinds. Almost half of all the different kinds of trees found in America grow in Florida. Some of Florida's woodlands are filled with majestic pine trees. Swamp maples, bald cypresses, bays, and oaks grow in some of the state's forests. Still other wooded areas are a mix of different types and species of plant life. Dozens of different kinds of subtropical trees can be found in the Florida peninsula and the Keys. The warm climate in these areas nourishes the strangler fig, royal palm, and mangroves, for example.

Main idea in the *middle* of a paragraph:

Business people are dressed neatly — the women in suits or skirts and blouses and the men in jackets, ties, pressed pants, and white shirts. Restaurant servers are polite to tourists and residents alike. Children stand quietly by their parents. <u>Almost all aspects of life on the island are polite and civilized.</u> People hold doors open for one another, wait to get into elevators until everyone has gotten off, and step aside to let those in a rush get by. At noon, the shops close and everyone goes home for a two-hour rest. But if you ask the shopkeepers to stay open a little longer, they will often gladly do so.

Main idea at the *end* of a paragraph:

The brown pelican, Florida's most popular bird, can often be seen perched on jetties, bridges, and piers. The state wetlands boast herons, egrets, wood ducks, and roseate spoonbills (often mistaken for flamingos). On the beach you can find sanderlings, plovers, and oystercatchers. The state bird, the mockingbird, likes living in suburban neighborhoods. Offshore, cormorants, black skimmers, and terns look for their dinner. Quail, wild turkey, owls, and woodpeckers live in Florida's forests. <u>In all, more than a hundred native species of birds have been found in Florida.</u>

Find the stated main idea in the following paragraph.

Tsunamis, or huge seismic sea-waves, are gravity waves set in motion by underwater disturbances associated with earthquakes. These waves are frequently called tidal waves although they have nothing to do with the tides. Near its origin, the first wave of a tsunami may be the largest; at greater distances, the largest is normally between the second and seventh wave.

You can find the stated main idea in the first sentence: "Tsunamis, or seismic sea-waves, are gravity waves set in motion by underwater disturbances associated with earthquakes."

Find an Unstated Main Idea

To find the unstated main idea in a paragraph, you have to make inferences, or educated guesses. Follow these steps:

1. Find the topic or subject of the paragraph.

2. Look for details that relate to the topic.

3. Make an educated guess about the main idea from the details.

Find the unstated main idea in the following paragraph.

Egypt, Land of the Pyramids

Egypt, a long, narrow, fertile strip of land in northeastern Africa, is the only place in the world where pyramids were built. Back then, all the water for the land and its people came from the mighty Nile River. Natural barriers protected the land from invaders. Around 300 B.C., when kings and other high Egyptian officials authorized the building of the first pyramids, these natural barriers protected the land from invaders. There were deserts to the east and west that cut off Egypt from the rest of the world. There were dangerous rapids on the Nile to the south. Delta marshes lay to the north. This isolation allowed the Egyptians to work in peace and security. In addition, great supplies of raw materials were needed to build the pyramids. Ancient Egypt had an abundance of limestone, sandstone, and granite. These rocks were cut close to the banks of the Nile. But these rocks had to be brought from quarries to the building sites. Egypt's most precious resource — the great Nile River — provided the means for transportation.

1. **Find the topic or subject of the paragraph**

   • *The pyramids of Egypt.*

2. **Look for details that relate to the topic**

   • *Natural barriers protected the land from invaders.*

   • *Ancient Egypt had the raw materials: limestone, sandstone, and granite.*

   • *Workers transported the stone on the Nile River.*

3. **Make an inference, or educated guess, about the main idea from the details**

   • *Ancient Egypt had a unique combination of ingredients necessary for building the pyramids.*

FIND KEY DETAILS

Like detectives, good readers look for clues to support their conclusions. These clues are *details,* words that tell who, what, when, where, why, and how. They are often called the *5W's and H*. Detectives know that finding the right clues can help them solve a mystery. Good readers know that finding the 5W's and H can help them understand and remember an author's most important points.

Details are small pieces of information that support the main idea. Details tell about people, events, things, time, objects, situations, or the way something happened. Details will fall into these six main categories:

1. Examples	Give specific information about the main idea.
2. Facts	Statements that can be proven.
3. Statistics	Numbers used to give additional information.
4. Reasons	Explanations that tell *why* something happened.
5. Definitions	Statements that explain what something means. Definitions often come from the dictionary.
6. Descriptions	Words or phrases that tell how something looks, smells, tastes, sounds, or feels. Descriptions help readers get a mental picture of what they are reading.

Follow these steps to find the key details in a paragraph:

Step 1: *Identify the topic*

Look for the subject of the paragraph.

Step 2: *Identify the main idea*

The *main idea* may be stated or unstated.

Step 3: *Find details that back up the main idea*

Look for the details that directly support the topic or main idea by telling who, what, when, where, why, or how.

T I P

Some paragraphs include details that answer who, what, where, when, why, and how, while other paragraphs provide less information.

Check your work by arranging the details you find on a web or chart under the headings *Who, What, Where, When, Why,* and *How.* Try it with the following passage.

Blue Jeans

In 1850, twenty-one-year-old Levi Strauss traveled from New York to San Francisco. Strauss had carried needles, thread, pots, pans, ribbons, yarn, scissors, buttons, and canvas across the country to sell to the gold miners. The small items sold well, but Strauss

Levi Strauss invented blue jeans almost by accident!

found himself stuck with the rolls of canvas because the canvas was not heavy enough to be used for tents. While talking to one of the miners, Strauss learned that sturdy pants that would stand up to the rigors of digging were almost impossible to find. For six dollars in gold dust, Strauss had a piece of the leftover canvas made into a pair of stiff but rugged pants. The miner was delighted with the result, and word got around about "those pants of Levi's." Business was so good that Strauss was soon out of canvas. He wrote to his brothers to send more. He received instead a tough brown cotton cloth called *serge de Nimes*. The foreign term was shortened to *denim*. Strauss had the cloth dyed a rich blue called indigo, which became a company trademark. These were the beginnings of a fashion that would become popular around the world.

Juan made the word web to show the details in the passage. A word web is a way to arrange the details in a passage or any writing.

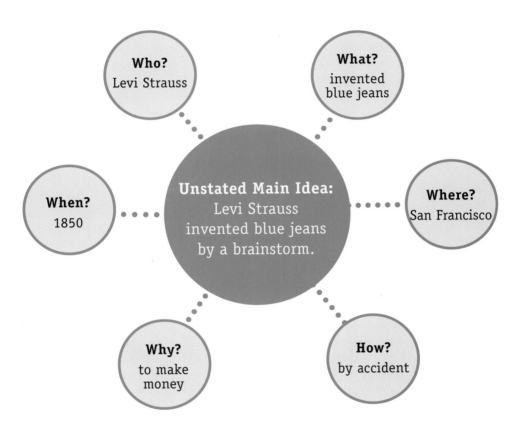

Now, infer the main idea of the following passage by finding the details:

Girl Scout National Centers

Girl Scouts from everywhere in the United States can meet other Girl Scouts at two special places called national centers. The Juliette Gordon Low Girl Scout National Center, also known as "The Birthplace," is the home in Savannah, Georgia, where Juliette Gordon Low was born. People can visit this historic house, museum, and program center and learn about Juliette Gordon Low's life. Girl Scout troops can take part in many educational and enjoyable activities. The other national

Today, more than 200,000 girls are involved in scouting on all levels.

center for Girl Scouts to meet is the Edith
Macy Conference Center, in Briarcliff Manor,
New York. Adults — not children — meet there
to learn more about Girl Scouts.

Here's the web Tamika made to find the unstated main idea from the
details in this passage:

SUMMARIZE WHAT YOU READ

To *summarize,* find the most important information and restate it in your own words. Summarize every time you study to help you understand and remember what you read. To be sure you have included all the important details in your summary, be sure that it answers these questions: Who? What? When? Where? Why? and How?

To summarize a passage . . .

1. preview the passage, set predictions, and read the passage.

2. find the main idea and important details.

3. explain them in your own words.

4. skim the passage again to make sure you have included all the important points.

5. begin your summary by stating the main idea. Then summarize the key details.

> **T I P**
>
> **A summary is shorter than the original passage. You can remember this because both *summary* and *shorter* start with *s.***

At first, you might stop to summarize after every paragraph or two. With practice, however, you should be able to summarize a page or two at a time. Summarize the following passage.

Keeping an Eye on the Weather

Ever hear the phrase, "Everybody always talks about the weather, but no one ever does anything about it"? Well, we do talk about the weather a lot, because it affects almost everything that we do. Of course, forecasters don't just look out the window to prepare the weather report you see on television. They use a weather information network located all over — and above — the planet. More than a dozen weather satellites orbit the Earth constantly. Other weather satellites remain in fixed positions 22,000 miles (35,406 kilometers) above the equator. Their rotating cameras can photograph the entire Earth, except for the North and South poles. The North and South poles are photographed by

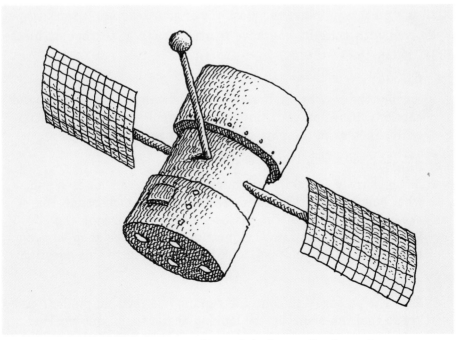

Weather forecasters use satellites to help them predict the weather.

additional satellites. Airplanes and balloons make daily ascents to gather data. Weather stations in almost every country on Earth contribute information for forecasters to use.

Here is Rosa's summary:

People really need and want to know about the weather. Orbiting and fixed satellites help experts predict the weather. The North and South poles are covered by special satellites. Airplanes and balloons also gather data. All over the world, weather stations send in facts about the weather.

USE SQ3R

SQ3R is a great way to get the most out of your reading. It works especially well with material you have to study, such as textbooks. To use SQ3R, follow these steps:

- **Survey**
  Preview the text by reading the title, headings, illustrations, and captions. Based on your survey, make predictions about the contents. Then skim the passage to get its overall meaning.

- **Question**
  As you survey and skim, ask questions about the material and what you find. Start by turning the title into a question. For example, look back at the passage "Keeping an Eye on the Weather." Turn this into the question "How do we keep an eye on the weather?" As you read, look for the answer to this question.

- **Read**
  Read the passage and continue making and revising predictions. Try to find the main idea by looking at the topic sentence and details in each paragraph.

- **Recite**

  After you finish reading, look back over the passage. Focus on the title, headings, and topic sentences. Summarize the material in your head, reducing what you read to a few sentences. Then recite or say your summary aloud.

- **Review**

  Review by looking back at your predictions. Were they on target? If so, find the details you used to make them. If not, figure out where and why you guessed incorrectly.

Try SQ3R with the following passage:

Jim Thorpe

Jim Thorpe (1888–1953) was a member of the 1912 U.S. Olympic Track and Field Team. He later played professional baseball and football.

In 1950, 400 American sportswriters and broadcasters selected Jim Thorpe as the greatest all-around athlete and football player of the first half of the 20th century. A Sac and Fox Indian, Thorpe was born in Oklahoma in 1888. Although he was a very good high school athlete, he stunned the entire world at the 1912 Olympic Games in Stockholm when he won gold medals in both the pentathlon and the decathlon. To date, no other athlete has ever duplicated his amazing achievement. A year later, the International Olympic Committee learned that Thorpe had accepted money in 1911 to play baseball. The

International Olympic Committee took away Thorpe's amateur status, took back his gold medals, and erased his achievements from the record books. Many people feel that Thorpe had been treated unfairly. In 1982, the International Olympic Committee restored Thorpe's amateur status and returned his medals.

Here's how one reader used SQ3R with this passage:

- **Survey**
  "Based on reading the title and heading, I predict that this paragraph will tell about the track, baseball, and football star Jim Thorpe."

- **Question**
  "I'll turn the title into these questions: Who was Jim Thorpe? Why is he important?"

- **Read**
  "I've read about halfway. I now predict that Jim Thorpe will get his Olympic medals back because he deserves them."

- **Recite**
  "Here's my summary: Jim Thorpe was an amazing athlete who got cheated out of his medals because he played baseball for money. Olympic athletes have to be amateurs, so they can't accept money for playing. Jim's medals were taken away because he broke the rules, but in 1982, his medals were returned to him."

- **Review**
  "I guessed correctly: Jim's medals were returned to him. I used the details about his amazing athletic abilities to make my guess. Someone that good can't get cheated!"

USE SMRR

Like SQ3R, SMRR combines many powerful reading techniques to give you a study boost. SMRR is especially good when you're studying a text, because you highlight important details. However, try both SQ3R and SMRR to decide which one works better for you. Here's how to use SMRR:

- **Skim**
  Preview the passage by scanning the title, heading, art, and captions. Then read the passage as quickly as you can.

- **Mark**
  Using a highlighter, pencil, or pen, mark the topic sentence and key details. Of course, never mark a text that doesn't belong to you!

- **Read**
  Read the text slowly and carefully, checking that you correctly identified the main idea and important points.

- **Reread**
  Go back over the text, checking that you understood the main idea.

USE CONTEXT CLUES

When people say "I can't read well," what they sometimes mean is "I get stuck on the hard words." You can always use a dictionary to figure out the hard word, but a dictionary isn't the only place you can find a word's meaning. Writers often leave hints, called *context clues,* in their stories to help readers figure out the difficult words.

Here are the main types of context clues:

Definition Clues

With this clue, the writer includes the definition right in the passage. The definition is a *synonym* (word that means the same). It may come before or after the unfamiliar word. For example:

> *Tsunamis,* or seismic sea-waves, are gravity waves set in motion by underwater disturbances associated with earthquakes.

Seismic sea-waves is a synonym for the unfamiliar word *tsunamis.*

Contrast Clues

With this clue, the writer tells you what something isn't rather than what it is. Often, you'll find contrast clues set off with *unlike, not,* or *instead of.* For example:

> Then arrange a handful of mulch, not fresh leaves, on the top.

Mulch must be the opposite of fresh leaves. It must mean "decayed leaves."

Commonsense Clues

With this clue, you use what you already know to define the word. One way is to break the unfamiliar word into its smaller words. Here is another way:

> Airplanes and balloons make daily *ascents* to gather data.

Since airplanes and balloons go into the air, *ascent* must mean "to rise."

> **TIP**
>
> Watch for *idioms*, phrases that don't have a literal meaning. The idiom "It's raining cats and dogs" means it's raining hard, not that cats and dogs are flying through the sky!

MONITOR YOUR COMPREHENSION

It can help to call a "time-out" when you're getting a little confused. Ask yourself, "What am I having trouble understanding?" Once you know, try some of the strategies below to get back on track.

Strategy Checklist

- Read more slowly.
- Reread any parts that confuse you.
- Look back at the pictures, charts, illustrations, and photographs.
- Use the details to visualize or imagine the scene you're reading.
- Restate what you've read in your own words.
- Ask yourself, "What is the main idea?" Reread the story for details and clues.
- Get some help. Use a reference book such as a dictionary to help you define words you don't know. Ask a teacher, friend, or parent to help you interpret a passage.

PREPARING FOR A TEST

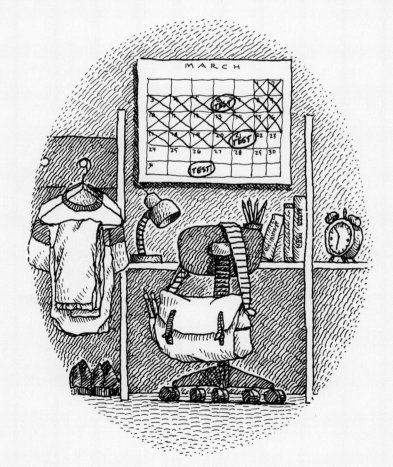

hen does the test start? When the teacher walks into the room? When the bell rings and the papers are handed out? When you start answering the test questions? Actually, the test starts long before you think.

Tests begin when you study and prepare for them! The groundwork takes place days before the actual test. To do your best on any test, you have to be ready. You'll learn how to prepare for a test in this section.

GET THE SCOOP!

Before you can prepare for a test, you have to know what you're preparing *for*! That's because each test is different. Knowing what to expect helps reduce test jitters, too. Here are some ways to find out what will be tested.

1. Start by asking your teacher.

   - Find out the test *format*. Will the test be true/false, multiple-choice, fill-in, essay, or some combination of the four?

   - Find out the test *content*. What information will you need to know?

   - Find out how much of the test is based on your notes, how much on the textbook, and how much on class work.

   - Listen to what the teacher says. Ask questions if you are confused.

2. Speak to other students in your class. See how they understand the instructions the teacher has given. This is a good way to check your comprehension, too.

3. You can also review tests you've already taken in this class. These tests will show you the types of questions the teacher asks. You'll find out what information the teacher stresses, too, so you can make sure you're on target when you study.

4. Pay close attention to the material the teacher writes on the board. Copy

it all down. Teachers write down the material they think is important, so you can be sure some or all of it will appear on a test.

5. Go to extra-help classes the teacher offers. Teachers often review for tests during these sessions.

However, if you're taking a standardized test, there's no "teacher" to ask. In these cases, you can request sample questions from the company that administers the test. Often, your teacher will have sample questions for the class to use. Usually, these sample questions will be given to you in a booklet when you sign up for the test. You can also find standardized test questions on-line at the test Web site. The address for the test Web site will be listed in the test booklet.

Organize and Review Notes

Now that you know what you'll be tested on, gather your textbook, notes, and flash cards. Arrange them in the order in which the material was presented. Highlight important ideas and focus on them.

Skim the textbook and take notes on any information you might be missing in your notes. Add this information to your notes. Be sure to review it as you study.

Use Review Material in the Textbook

Many textbooks contain review questions at the end of each section or chapter. Even if the teacher hasn't assigned these questions, answer them as you prepare for the test. You can find the answers by going back over the chapter. When you look for the answers, you are also rereading the chapter.

PRACTICE MAKES PERFECT

To make the most of your study time, get into a study routine. Try these hints:

• Study at the same time every day in the same place. Sit at your desk in your study center to get into the study habit.

- Study your most difficult material first, when you're least tired.

- Use the memory techniques you learned in Section One to fix important concepts and ideas in your mind.

- As you study, give yourself short breaks. Stretch every 15 minutes or so.

Practice on similar tests to find out your strengths and weaknesses. For example, if you have trouble writing an essay in the time you have, concentrate on learning this skill. (Taking essay tests is covered in detail in Section Five.) Completing similar tests also helps you learn how to make the best use of your time.

> **T I P**
>
> **Don't take real standardized tests "just for practice," because they go on your permanent record. Instead, practice with previously published standardized tests, available in review books.**

If you don't have enough old tests to use because it's early in the year, make up your own tests. Use the material for the upcoming test. You can trade tests with a homework buddy or a small group of classmates to increase your "test bank."

STUDY ALONE OR IN GROUPS

Studying with classmates can help you in many ways. Group members can take turns summarizing the material aloud or quizzing one another on important topics. Some group members ask questions to help clear up confusing points while other group members provide the answers. Group members can pass around their notes, too, which helps fill in gaps in everyone's notes. Since everyone looks at a topic in his or her unique way, group members can help you see the readings and class notes from different angles.

Some people study in groups, but others prefer to work alone. For example, Samantha likes to study in a group because she feels it helps her review the material more completely. Lawrence, however, avoids study groups because he finds that he's always doing more work than his friends. The following chart shows some of the advantages and disadvantages of studying in groups:

STUDY GROUPS

Advantages	Disadvantages
build confidence for some students	waste time if you're prepared and others aren't
give you a chance to review material you might have missed	cause insecurity or panic for some students
can help you focus	can be very distracting

Studying in groups may be right for you if you can concentrate on your work even if others go off track. Group study is also helpful if you've missed some classes and don't understand all the information. Avoid group work if you find it hard to stay on track in groups or realize that your friends don't do their share of the work. In addition, group study might not work for you if you often measure your progress against others and find yourself coming up short.

> **TIP**
>
> **Study groups are most effective when they're small, no more than three to five students.**

TO CRAM OR NOT TO CRAM?

Soccer practice. A new puppy. A big party. Help! You're pressed for time. Why not leave all your studying to the last minute and cram it all in? Here's why not — cramming doesn't work. It also tends to make you panic when you realize that there's no way you can learn a week's worth of information in an hour.

Instead of wasting your time cramming, try this effective study plan:

POWER STUDY PLAN

Four days before the test	Reread your notes and the textbook.
Three days before the test	Skim your notes and the textbook. Recite important points aloud.
Two days before the test	Without looking at your notes or the textbook, recite the key points. Look back at your notes and the text to check your success.
The day before the test	Make a sample test and answer the questions or have someone quiz you. Skim your notes and the textbook to find the most important points.
The day of the test	If the test is in the morning, you may not be able to study. If you do have a few minutes, however, skim your notes one last time. Be sure to relax before the test!

TIP **If you're taking a nationwide standardized test, you need identification to get into the test room. Be sure to have a valid photo ID or passport, or you won't even be admitted to the test.**

ON YOUR MARK, GET SET, GO!

There's even more you can do to increase your chances of success on any test. Try these strategies to become a super test taker:

1. **Prepare the night before**
   Lay out your clothing, pens or pencils, watch, lunch, and other school supplies. You don't want to be rushing around in the morning.

2. Choose comfortable clothing

Avoid itchy sweaters or starchy pants. Your clothes should be loose enough so that you feel comfortable.

3. Get a good night's sleep

Yes, I know you've heard it before, but it really works. A solid eight hours of *zzzz*'s can recharge your batteries and give you the winning edge on *any* test.

4. Be sure to eat breakfast

Eat a nourishing breakfast of cereal, fruit, and toast. You might want to have eggs, French toast, or pancakes. Don't make do with a toaster pastry or doughnut.

5. Avoid soda

Too much caffeine can give you the jitters, so avoid caffeinated colas. (Besides, you shouldn't be drinking soda for breakfast!)

6. Wake up!

If you're a morning sleepyhead, wake yourself up with a hot shower or brief exercise. A short jog works well (and you can walk the dog at the same time).

7. Leave yourself enough time in the morning

Figure out how much time you need in the morning to get ready — and then add an extra 15 minutes. If an emergency arises, you'll have time to deal with it. If everything goes smoothly, you can review your notes for a few extra minutes.

8. Build your self-confidence

Getting yourself all upset before a big test will make you feel more nervous. It can also rob you of the confidence you need to succeed. Remind yourself that you have prepared well so you will do well. A positive attitude brings great results.

CALM TEST JITTERS

"All we have to fear is fear itself," said President Franklin Delano Roosevelt. President Roosevelt was right, but try telling that to all the butterflies in your stomach the night before a big test!

It's natural to feel nervous before a high-pressure situation; in fact, some scientists think tension under pressure comes from ancient days when we faced bison and other gigantic creatures. How can you relieve test anxiety *before* the test? Try these strategies:

- Be prepared, as you learned above. Studying your notes in detail can help you feel confident. Knowing what's going to be on the test and the form it will take can go a long way to reducing test anxiety, too.

- Exercise to reduce tension. Even 10 minutes of jogging can take off the edge.
- Imagine the teacher handing back your test with a big "A" on top. Visualizing success puts you in control.

TEST-TAKING SKILLS

ou've read all your textbooks, listened carefully in class, taken notes, and reviewed your notes. Perhaps you've studied with a group of friends, too. You've certainly made up your own test questions to test your knowledge of the material.

It's not enough to know the material, however; you also have to know how to take tests. Knowing a few simple test-taking strategies can earn you higher grades. You'll learn these super test-taking techniques in this part of the book.

BEFORE THE TEST

When you compete in a race, you try to get a running start. You know that if you start out in the lead, it's easier to stay ahead of the pack. The same is true when you take a test. Here's how to start off on the right foot.

Be Prepared

Be sure to have everything you need for the test: pens, pencils, erasers, calculators, rulers, and so on. Since you put all these materials in your backpack the night before, you should be well prepared on the day of the test. Grab your backpack and you're all set to test!

Arrive at the Test Early

Get to the classroom with time to spare. Allow yourself enough time to settle in the seat, lay out your pens and pencils, and relax. If you're sitting in your chair early with everything set to go, you'll have time to calm down and focus on the task at hand, too. Be sure to leave yourself at least five extra minutes so you're not dashing in at the last minute, huffing and puffing!

Choose Your Seat Carefully

Sitting near friends during a test can be disrupting. If you see your friends handing in their papers early, you may feel pressure to do the same, even if you're not finished with the test. Therefore, if you are allowed to choose your seat, try not to sit near your friends. Choose a seat in the front of the room, so you can clearly see and hear the teacher.

Also, stay away from people who read the questions aloud to themselves, chew gum and crack it loudly, or play with their pens and pencils as they take tests. These distractions can make it difficult for you to concentrate.

> **T**
> **I**
> **P**
>
> **Always carry extra batteries for your calculator. Calculators (and other battery-operated study aids such as electronic spell checkers) have a nasty habit of running out of battery power just when you need them the most.**

Calm Down!

Since you've arrived at the test early and you're fully prepared for success, you should be relaxed. If you still have some last-minute jitters, take a few deep breaths and focus on a pleasant scene. Imagine being at the lake, beach, or park, for example.

Remind yourself that you are well prepared for this test, because you *are*. Convince yourself that other students have aced this test and you can, too.

Keeping yourself focused can also reduce tension. Try not to think about anything but the test in front of you. If you find your mind wandering, return to the test — but don't forget to pat yourself on the back for staying in control. Focusing on the test again shows that you've stopped yourself from wasting time.

Pay Close Attention to All Directions — Spoken and Written

The test directions will usually be given orally and in writing. The teacher or proctor will announce some directions after everyone has settled down, and then direct students to read the directions written on the test. Pay very close attention to what is said and what you read because following the directions closely can make the difference between a high grade or a low one.

> **T I P**
>
> **Be sure to check the chalkboard before you start a test. The teacher might have written some important directions or the test time on the board.**

As you read the directions, pay close attention to what you must do. Ask yourself these questions as you read:

- "How many questions do I have to answer?" On some tests you have to answer all the questions; on other tests, only a few. For example, if you overlook the sentence "Choose one of the four possible essay topics" and you try to write all four essays, you'll probably run out of time and give incomplete answers.

- "Where do I have to write my answers?" You might have a special answer sheet, a test booklet, or your own paper.

- "Will I lose points for guessing?" The teacher might subtract points for incorrect answers. If there is no penalty for guessing, never leave an answer blank. More information later on guessing.

- "How much information do I have to include?" You might have to show every step in a math problem, for example, or include four paragraphs in your essay.

If you still have questions after the teacher speaks and you have read all the directions, raise your hand and get the answers you need. Be sure you completely understand the directions before you plunge into the test.

> **If you are taking a standardized test such as a state assessment, memorize the directions beforehand. Teachers give practice versions of these tests, so you will have many chances to learn the directions. On test day, quickly skim the directions to make sure they are the same. You can often save as much as 10 minutes this way!**

Budget Your Time

Before you start working on the test, figure out how much each part of the test counts. On some tests, every question is worth the same number of points. All the questions might be worth 1 point each, 4 points each, or 5 points each, for instance. On other tests, however, some sections may be worth more points than others.

For instance, the first section may have 10 questions that count for 1 point each (for a total of 10 points), the second section may have 20 questions that count for 3 points each (for a total of 60 points), and the third section may have an essay that counts for 30 points. The amount that each question or section is worth should affect the time you spend on each part of the test.

HERE'S THE RULE:

Spend the most time on the sections that count the most. Spend the least time on sections that count the least.

You should avoid spending too much time on one question. Before you begin your test, make a plan for budgeting your time. For example, if you have 90 minutes and 100 short-answer items, spend about 1 minute on each question. If you have 1 hour and 100 short-answer items, spend about 30 seconds on each question.

If you don't complete a question in the time you have allotted, leave it and move on. You can return to the question if you have extra time at the end of the test. If you do skip a question and move on, *be very careful to mark your answer sheet correctly.*

You also have to budget your time if you are writing an essay. Decide how much time you can spend planning, drafting, and revising. Don't make yourself nervous trying to stick to your schedule, but do keep an eye on the time and try to stay on track. For a half-hour writing exam, for instance, you can spend about 3 minutes planning what you're going to write, 15 minutes writing, 10 minutes revising and editing, and 2 to 3 minutes proofreading to catch any errors.

If you have time left over, spend it . . .

- double-checking your answers.
- returning to questions you could not answer the first time.
- proofreading your essay for errors in grammar, usage, and punctuation.
- recopying messy parts of your essays.

DURING THE TEST
Identify Yourself!

As soon as you have read the directions and skimmed the entire test, write your name, date, and class on the paper. Also include any other information the teacher wants, such as your homeroom, address, or age. It's amazing how many test papers get turned in without names. Identifying yourself is especially important on state assessments, which may not be marked by your own teacher. As a result, the grader will not know your handwriting or writing style and so won't be able to identify you.

If the teacher can't identify your paper, your "A" might be given to another student by mistake!

Read the Entire Test Before You Start Answering Questions

Before you start writing, take a few minutes to skim the test. Remember, when you skim a passage, you read it very quickly to get the main idea. Here's what to look for:

- The types of questions (short-answer, true/false, etc.)
- The content of the questions
- Which questions look easy and which ones look difficult

Knowing what's on the test helps you develop a test strategy (explained on p. 81). It also reassures you that you studied the right material and are well prepared for the test.

Jot Down Notes and Key Facts

As soon as you have written your name and skimmed the entire test, write down any important details or facts while they are still fresh in your memory. These notes may help you answer questions later on. In addition, having some notes reduces test anxiety because it reminds you that you have learned a lot.

Depending on the test content, here are some notes you may wish to jot down:

- Multiplication tables
- Math formulas
- Science facts
- Key historical dates and events
- Important fictional characters or real-life people
- Literary terms, such as *rhyme, simile,* and *metaphor*
- Geographical places and features (lakes, rivers, oceans, etc.)
- Foreign language words and their definitions
- Vocabulary words and their meanings
- Spelling words

Write your notes on scrap paper, inside the test booklet, or in the test margins. Always be sure that you can write in these places before you do. After all, you don't want your notes being counted as an answer!

Get a Test Strategy

There are three ways you can approach any test:

1. Work from beginning to end, answering every question in order. Answer every single question, even if you have to guess.

2. Answer the easy questions first, and then go back and work on the harder questions.

3. Answer the hardest questions first, and then go back and answer the easy ones.

None of these test-taking methods is right or wrong, but for most people, method 2 works best. Therefore, you should answer the easier questions first and then go back to figure out the more difficult ones. This strategy helps you in many ways:

- You use your time well by getting the most correct answers down fast.

- You build confidence as you write down the correct answers.

- You often think of clues that help you answer the more difficult questions.

- You may find the correct answer to a hard question revealed in another test question.

- You build momentum, which gets your mind into the test mode.

- You leave time for the harder questions.

- You reduce any penalty you might have for guessing (more on this later).

How can you determine which questions are simple and which ones are complex? Questions can be easy or hard based on two factors: their *content* and their *form*.

- *Content* refers to the subject, the information the question tests.
- *Form* refers to the type of question, such as true/false, fill in the blank, or essay questions.

You judge the *content* based on the material you studied. For example, if you are being tested on state capitals and you have memorized them all, then the test content will be easy for you. But if you are being asked to factor equations and you did not study this topic, the content will be very challenging.

The following chart can help you judge how difficult a question is based on its *form*.

QUESTION FORM AND LEVEL OF DIFFICULTY

Easier	More Difficult	Most Difficult
multiple-choice	fill-in-the-blank	essays
matching	sentence completion	
true/false	short answer	

It's best to tackle the easiest questions first. Therefore, answer all the true/false, multiple-choice, and matching questions you can before you move on to fill-in-the-blank, sentence completion, and short-answer questions. Leave the essay questions for last. Of course, you have already allocated your time, so you know how much to spend on each question.

As you work from the beginning to the end, put a checkmark next to any question you skip. Write in pencil so you can erase the checkmarks in case you are not allowed to write on the test. When you get to the end of the test, go back to the beginning and start answering the questions you skipped.

If you are allowed to write on the test, use a highlighter to underline important material. You can also make notes or write arrows in the margin to point out important facts.

When you take multiple-choice tests, cross out any answer choices you know are wrong. This helps you eliminate wrong answers.

> **T**
> **I**
> **P**
>
> **Keep moving so you stay within your time limit. Never let yourself spend too much time on one or two questions, especially if they are not worth many points.**

Read the Questions Carefully

Imagine that you come to question 25. It's a multiple-choice question with four choices, A, B, C, D. You read the question and choice A. *Ah-ha!* you think. *The correct choice is clearly A.* Should you write A on your answer sheet? No!

Even if you think you have spotted the correct answer immediately, read every single answer to make sure that you are correct. You might have misread the question; this is a common mistake. People tend to see what they expect, not what is really on the page. This is especially true in a high-pressure situation such as a test. Take a close look at every choice before you make your decision and mark your answer.

Ask for Clarification

What happens when you read a question over several times and it just doesn't make sense? You skip the question and move on. When you return to the question, however, it still doesn't make any sense, so you read it for a third time. It's still murky.

If you really don't understand a question and you've read it over several times, raise your hand and ask the teacher or proctor for clarification. In most cases, the teacher will be able to point you in the right direction. In other cases, however, the teacher may not be allowed to offer you any assistance. This is especially true on standardized tests. In these instances, you will have to do the best you can by analyzing the test question. Read on to find out some ways to do this.

> **T I P**
>
> **Never ask a fellow classmate to clarify a question for you. If you do, the teacher or proctor may think you are cheating. Speak only to the teacher or person administering the test.**

Don't Second-Guess Yourself

"The short-answer pattern really matters," some people say. "You can never have two C's (or A's, B's, and so on) in a row," you may have heard. Not true! The pattern of letters on the answer sheet doesn't matter at all. You may have an ABCDABCD pattern, an AABBCCDD pattern, any other pattern, or no pattern at all. It never matters.

If you do see a pattern, don't be fooled into changing your answers. Your grade will always be higher if you answer questions based on what you know rather than the way the answers look on the page. If you start to think that you've chosen the incorrect answer, analyze the question rather than the answer pattern. If you can't think of a good reason to change the answer, leave it alone. Studies show that your first choice is more often the correct one.

Be Creative, but Don't "Overthink"

Sometimes the answer isn't obvious. This may be the case with word analogy questions, for example. When you complete a word analogy question, you are looking for a relationship between pairs of words. You have to find the answer choice that best matches the relationship between the words in capital letters. For example:

OBVIOUS ANSWER	OBSCURE ANSWER
SHOE: FOOT	**ACT: PLAY**
A. nose: ear	A. line: music
B. shirt: arm	B. page: novel
C. toes: foot	C. scenery: performance
D. glove: hand	D. chapter: book
E. hat: knee	

The correct answer is D:
A glove covers your hand as a shoe covers your foot. A is silly because a nose doesn't cover your ear. B is wrong because a shirt covers your entire torso, not just your arm. C is wrong because toes don't cover your foot; they are part of it. E is wrong because a hat covers your head, not your knee.

The correct answer is D:
An act is a large part of a play as a chapter is a large part of a book. A line is part of music and a page is part of a novel, but neither are large parts, so A and B can't be correct answers. C is wrong because scenery is not a part of a play.

To find the relationship between these words, you have to think creatively. Perhaps you put the words in a sentence, such as "Album is to photographs as . . ." Maybe you drew a diagram to find the relationship. You looked at the question from several different angles to analyze it. You have to use creative thinking skills on many tests.

But when you think creatively, be sure not to "overthink." When you "overthink," you analyze your answers so deeply that you create relationships that don't really exist. You might get hopelessly lost, too.

When in doubt, go for the most logical and obvious answer. If that doesn't fit, look more deeply into the question and see if you can find an answer that matches your line of thought.

Should You Guess?

Some tests penalize you for guessing, while others do not. In general, many standardized tests try to discourage guessing by taking off points for incorrect answers. The PSAT, SAT I, and SAT II tests take off points for guessing.

If there is *no* penalty for guessing, fill in every single answer — even if you have to guess. After all, you have nothing to lose and everything to gain! Most state assessments do not penalize you for guessing.

If there *is* a penalty for guessing, try to reduce the odds. For example, if every multiple-choice question gives you four possible answers, you have a 25 percent chance of being right (and a 75 percent chance of being wrong) each time you have to guess. But if you can eliminate a single answer, your chance of being correct rises to 33 percent. And if you can get your choices down to two answers, you have a 50 percent chance of being right. Even if there is a penalty for guessing, pick one answer if you can reduce your choices to two. Fifty percent odds are good enough to chance a guess.

Before you give up on any question, always try to eliminate one or more of the answer choices. Cross them off. Remember: The more choices you can eliminate, the better your odds of choosing the right answer.

Pace Yourself to Avoid Making Careless Errors

Make sure you are wearing a watch or can see a clock. This will help you keep working at the right pace. You want to work quickly, but not so quickly that you throw away points by working carelessly. It's an awful feeling to lose points on questions that you really can answer. There are several ways you can carelessly answer a question wrong:

- Misread a question
- Miscalculate a math problem
- Mark an answer wrong. (You mean to mark C but mark B instead because you're working too fast.)

- Skip a question, but *not* a space on the answer sheet

To prevent these careless errors, after you fill in your answers, check the answer sheet against the choices on the test. Read the answer and the letter to yourself. Say the letter in your head.

When you are working on math problems, check that your answers make sense. Are they logical? For example, if you are figuring a discount, make sure that it's not more than the original price. If you're calculating the average age of a fourth grader, make sure it's not 65 years old!

Check and Double-Check Your Work

When you finish the test, always check your work. Even if you have just a minute or two, use your time to look over your papers.

Ask yourself these questions as you check fill-in-the-blank, short-answer, and essay tests:

- Have I included all necessary words? People often omit words when they are in a hurry.

- Have I spelled all the words correctly? Check easy words as well as more difficult ones.

- Is my punctuation correct?

- Have I checked my grammar and usage?

- Can my writing be read easily?

> **T I P**
>
> **If your writing is difficult to read, consider printing. Don't use all block capitals, however. Instead, use the accepted mix of uppercase and lowercase letters.**

Ask yourself these questions as you check short-answer tests:

- Have I filled in my responses on the correct places on the answer sheet?

- If I am not being penalized for guessing, did I fill in each blank?

- If I had to bubble in circles, are my responses neat?

- If I had to write letters or numbers, can my answers be read easily?

- On standardized tests, did I erase any stray marks that might be misread?

Losing your place on an answer sheet is a major disaster that should never happen. Here's how it happens:

- You're working from the beginning to the end of the test. You get stuck on a few test items, so you skip them and keep on working.

- You focus on the next question and forget to skip a space on the answer sheet. As a result, you bubble in the correct answer — but in the wrong spot.

- When you get to the last spot on the answer sheet, you have two spaces left. You suddenly realize that when you skipped the questions, you forgot to skip the spaces on the answer sheet — even though you put checkmarks next to the questions!

You can avoid this disaster by checking your answer sheet each time you skip a question. Keeping your answer sheet next to the test booklet can help you remember to keep checking.

Time Issues

You know that you have to pace yourself to do your best. But did you also know that you can improve your score by taking a short break if you feel you're losing your concentration? Look up from the test, stretch, and take a few deep breaths. Often, just a brief pause — a minute or two — can refresh you and give you a "second wind."

Also, be sure to use all the time you have been given, every single minute. You should never turn your paper in and leave early. Check your work over and think about your answers. If you are sure you're completely done, set your test aside and take a brief break. A few minutes later, look back at the test and your answers. Errors often pop right out when you've stepped away from the test. You don't want to be out the door and suddenly realize that you have finished so early because you forgot to write one of the essays!

> **Reread the test questions and compare your answers against them. This will help you make sure that you have answered every part of each question.**

Dealing with Panic

Panic is a natural reaction to a pressure situation. Nonetheless, panic can prevent you from doing your best on tests, so let's reduce or banish it. Here are some techniques that can help you deal with panic:

Don't panic if . . .

- **some questions seem much harder than others.**
  They probably are! That's the way the test was designed. This is especially true on state tests and other standardized tests. Accept this and do the best you can. On standardized tests, you don't have to answer each question to do well. That's because you're not being marked against yourself; rather, you're being judged against all other test takers. They're feeling the same way you are.

- **other students are writing and you're not.**
  They may be working on another part of the test or not have thought enough. By thinking a bit longer before you answer, you might do better than someone who plunges right in.

- **other students finish before you do.**
  Finishing early doesn't guarantee the best grade. Usually the better papers are handed in by students who have spent more time thinking about their answers and checking over their papers.

- **you can't get an answer.**
  Just skip the question and move on. If you have enough time, you can return to the question later. If you run out of time before you can return to it, you are still better off answering more questions than wasting time on a question you don't know.

- **you run out of time.**
  You might be able to stay a little later to finish. If not, be confident that you studied, prepared, and did your best.

- **you blow the test all out of proportion.**
  It is true that some tests are more important than others, especially standardized state tests. But any test is only one factor in your overall education. Remind yourself that you have been working hard in class and keeping up with all your homework. Keep in mind that how you do on one test will not affect your entire academic career.

- **you freeze and just can't go on.**
  If this happens, there are many different things that you can do. Use the 3R's to banish panic:

  - **R**emind yourself that you have studied and so you are well prepared.

  - **R**emember that every question you have answered is worth points.

  - **R**eassure yourself that you're doing just fine. After all, you are!

As you use the 3R's, stop working and close your eyes. Take two or three deep breaths. Breathe in and out to the count of five. Then go on with the test.

AFTER THE TEST

After you complete the test, use it to improve for next time. If you got an "A," congratulations! If you didn't get the top grade, don't despair. Instead, use this as a learning experience. Don't compare yourself to your friends and classmates. Instead, focus on the things you did well to prepare and take the test. Remind yourself that next time you'll do better.

Here are some ways to get the most from your test-taking experience:

Evaluate What You Did Right and What You Can Do Better

With each test you take, you can become a better test taker — if you analyze your strengths and weaknesses. Think of yourself as an athlete in training. You practice and work out, but you can improve if you study your performance in detail. Here are some questions you can ask yourself:

- **What was my biggest problem on this test? How do I know?**
  You can figure out your biggest problem by seeing which questions you missed. Look for a pattern of errors. Perhaps you missed all the mathematical word problems or had trouble writing a logical and clear essay.

- **What caused my mistakes? For example, did I run out of time? Did I misread questions? Did I study the wrong material or not study carefully? Was I rushing? Did I make careless mistakes?**
  Look back at the pattern of errors and think what caused them. Be honest with yourself; take responsibility for your future.

- **How can I overcome this problem?**
  Perhaps you decide to take practice tests to learn how to make better use of your time. You might practice the reading comprehension techniques you learned in Section Two. Or you might decide to work with a study group to make sure you cover all the important information you may be missing on your own.

Check for Grading Errors

Teachers sometimes make mistakes when they grade tests. Perhaps the teacher misread your answer, seeing a *B* for a *D*. Or you might have solved the math problem in a different way and the teacher didn't understand what you were doing. There might even be a poorly designed question that has two valid answers.

Don't bother the teacher to get points that you really don't deserve. But do talk to the teacher if you think your test may have been misgraded. You may be able to get a higher score if you can show that your answer is correct or even reasonable.

Or, your teacher might be willing to give you additional credit for a partially correct answer. That's why it's important to show your work in math and science problems. If you're not allowed to show your work on the answer sheet or the test booklet, show it on the scrap paper. Be sure to turn the scrap paper in with the answer sheet.

Talk with Your Teacher

Most teachers really want to help their students succeed. This is even more true if you are clearly putting effort into your work. Teachers know that how well you learn depends in part on your attitude: If you approach school in a positive way, you're far more likely to do well when you study and take tests. When your teacher helps you, you'll feel more connected to your education.

Ask your teacher to evaluate your test to point out your strengths and weaknesses. See what suggestions your teacher makes. Compare these to what you have figured out on your own. If they match, you know where you have to put your effort. If they don't, look back at the test and see why there's a difference of opinion. Are you being honest with yourself?

Study Smarter

Adjust your study methods based on your self-assessment, your test score, and your teacher's advice. For example, if you find that your notes were weak, you might want to take notes in a different way. If you've been jotting down ideas, you might want to try making outlines. You can also photocopy your textbook and then highlight key points. Write comments in the margins, too.

If you find that you lost points because of careless errors, you can practice working more carefully and checking your work. If you got a lower score than you expected because you really didn't understand the

questions on the test, you should go for extra help. Misunderstandings have a way of getting worse.

   If you don't understand the material on this test, you're going to have a hard time building on it for the following test . . . and the one after that.

Get Some Help

For years, you've been doing great studying on your own. Suddenly, you find that your math grade is in the basement because you just don't understand the material. If you've tried the teacher's extra help and you're still confused, ask a friend to tutor you until you grasp the concept. If your friend isn't a math whiz, find out if your school has a tutoring service. Many schools have student tutors who work for free as part of their community service. You might be able to get extra help from your parents, relatives, and older brothers and sisters, too.

Plan for Next Time

Right now, you might feel like crumpling the test paper into a tight ball and throwing it into the garbage. Even though you're frustrated, don't give up. Tests are designed to see how well you know a specific subject. Think of the test in a positive way and you'll get more from the experience. Use what you learned to be the best student you can be.

It takes courage to learn from a painful experience, but you've come this far already. You're in the home stretch. With a bit more effort, you can raise your grade. Hard work and a positive attitude can pay off!

MASTERING SPECIFIC TESTS

Now that you know there are techniques for taking tests successfully, you're ready for the details. In this chapter, you'll learn some ways to avoid being trapped by tricky test questions. Use these skills to boost your grades on short-answer tests and essay tests.

SUPER SHORT-ANSWER TEST HINTS
Tips for True/False Test Questions

True/false questions require you to recognize a fact or idea. They also check your reading comprehension. As a result, you have to read very carefully and closely.

- **Pay close attention to absolute words.**
  When you take true/false tests, pay special attention to "absolute words." These are words that are all positive or all negative. Here are some examples:

  always   all   all the time   constantly   everyone

  never   none   not at all   no one   absolutely not

  You know that answers are rarely *always* or *never, black* or *white*. If you see an absolute word in a test item, the item will probably not be the correct answer. This is especially the case with true/false test items. For example:

  Directions: Circle *true* if the sentence is true or *false* if it is false.

  True False 1. A sentence fragment is never acceptable in writing.

  True False 2. Water always freezes at 32° Fahrenheit.

  Each of these items is false because of the absolute words *never* and *always*. Item 1 is false because sentence fragments are acceptable in dialogue and casual writing. Item 2 is false because water that contains salt will not freeze at 32° Fahrenheit. Adding salt to water lowers the temperature it needs to freeze.

Look for the words *usually, many, most, rarely, sometimes, generally,* and *frequently* in true/false test items. They will usually make a statement valid since they are not absolutes.

- **Study sentence length.**
  For a sentence to be true, all parts of it must be true. If even one small part is false, the entire sentence is false. Therefore, the longer a sentence, the more likely it is to be false. Pay very close attention to long sentences in true/false questions. Read every part to make sure that every word is true.

- **Be on your guard for false logic.**
  Two sentences can be true but connected by a word that makes them false. Look closely at the connecting word to make sure it doesn't make false connections. Here are some words and phrases used to connect sentences:

and	but	because	since	for	nor	or
yet	on account of	still	further	due to		

  For example: *President Abraham Lincoln is famous because he was assassinated by John Wilkes Booth.* Abraham Lincoln is famous and he was assassinated by John Wilkes Booth but that's not what made him famous. The connecting word *because* makes the sentence false.

- **Consider guessing.**
  When it comes to true/false questions, you should guess on all questions you can't answer, unless there is a penalty for guessing. Since you have a 50 percent chance of getting the answer right, take the chance.

Tips for Multiple-Choice Test Questions

Multiple-choice tests require you to choose the correct answer from several options. You may have three, four, or five choices. Multiple-choice tests are most difficult if the choices are very close in meaning.

- **Look for the words *not, except,* and *best.***

  Multiple-choice questions can snare you on the words *not, except,* or *best.* The questions will be phrased like this:

  Which is *not* an example of . . .

  All the following choices are correct *except* . . .

  The *best* answer is . . .

  These questions are tricky because you're being asked to choose an answer that's the opposite of what you expect. Here are some examples:

  3. Which is *not* a source in which you would be likely to find facts about the speed of light?

     A. science textbook

     B. encyclopedia

     C. travel brochure

     D. educational Web site

  4. When you solve a problem, you follow every step *except*

     A. defining the problem

     B. thinking of different solutions

     C. testing different solutions

     D. ignoring facts and outside information

Item 3 is choice C; item 4 is choice D. In item 3, science textbooks, encyclopedias, and educational Web sites would all most likely include facts about the speed of light. A travel brochure would contain facts about a vacation spot, but no information about the speed of light. In item 4, you define the problem, think of different solutions, and test those solutions when you solve a problem. You can't ignore facts and outside information, because these often have a great influence on the solution you come up with.

- **Watch the *all of the above* choice.**
  For the answer to be *all of the above*, every part of every choice has to be correct. Verify the truth of every part of every choice before you select *all of the above* as the correct choice.

Tips for Matching Test Questions

Matching tests assess your ability to see which things go together. Thinking of these tests like a puzzle will help you match the correct pieces and eliminate choices as you go along.

- **Read the list on the right first.**
  The questions will be listed on the left; the answers will be listed on the right. Read the answers (the right-hand column) first, so you know the answer choices. As you read down the list, you will know all the options. This can prevent you from choosing the first or second choice because it looks right, when the real answer is further down the list.

- **As you find each correct match, cross it off the list.**
  This helps you limit your choices and increase your chances of getting every answer correct.

Try it yourself with this sample test. Match the word to its definition.

____	1. desert	a. very flat land
____	2. hill	b. a building or statue built in honor of a person or event
____	3. island	c. a drawing of a place
____	4. monument	d. a dry place with little rain
____	5. mountain	e. land surrounded by water on three sides
____	6. ocean	f. land that rises above the land around it
____	7. peninsula	g. low land between hills or mountains
____	8. plain	h. land completely surrounded by water
____	9. valley	i. a very large body of salt water
____	10. map	j. the highest kind of land

Did you get these answers?

1. d   2. f   3. h   4. b   5. j
6. i   7. e   8. a   9. g   10. c

Tips for Fill-in-the-Blank Questions

You may or may not have answer choices with fill-in-the-blank questions. If you don't, you will have to recall the correct answer from the material you studied. If you do have answer choices, you will have to eliminate some answers and choose the best choice.

- **Look for links in ideas.**
  As you read the sentence, substitute the word *blank* for the blank. This helps you figure out what is missing and how the sentence makes sense when complete. If you have been given answer choices, try to predict the answer without looking at the

choices. Then look at the answer choices to find the one that best matches your prediction. If you haven't been given choices, fill in the answer based on your prediction. Here's an example:

A _____ is a person who comes from a country to live in a different land.

a. suburb   c. state

b. settler   d. leader

The correct answer is b. Choice a is wrong because a suburb is a community just outside a city. Choice c is wrong because a state is a part of a country. Choice d is wrong because a settler may be a leader, but doesn't have to be.

- **Look for context clues.**
  A sentence completion question usually contains clues to the correct answer. For example, the words *and, also, so, for, because,* and *therefore* show that the second part of the sentence supports the first part. When you see one of these words in a sentence comple-

tion question, look for answer choices that support the second part of the sentence.

Other times, the blank requires a word that restates an idea already mentioned in the sentence. In this case, you will be using *summary clues* to find the missing words. The following phrases show that ideas are being summarized: *as a result, in summary, finally, in conclusion.*

Finally, words such as *although, not, but,* and *however* signal contrast. If you see one of these words in the sentence, the missing word will be the opposite of the first half of the sentence.

- **Read carefully.**
  One letter can change the meaning of a word, so read each answer choice carefully.

  Dessert and *desert,* for instance, may look the same if you're reading fast, but they're not the same! *Dessert* is a sweet served at the end of a meal while *desert* is a very dry area of land.

- **Check capitalization.**
  Some words have two meanings, depending on whether or not they are capitalized. For example, when capitalized, the word *Catholic* refers to a religion. However, when *catholic* is written with a lower-case "c," it means "worldly, cosmopolitan, or wide-ranging tastes and interests."

- **Match the grammatical form of the question and answer.**
  If the verb is singular, the subject or answer must be singular. If the verb is plural, the subject or answer must be plural.

- **Check your answer by reading the entire sentence.**
  Rereading the answer you've chosen or written can help you decide if it makes sense. If not, revise your answer.

- **Use common sense to make sure your answer is logical.**
  If your answer doesn't match what you already know, revise it.

An answer can be true and still be wrong. The correct choice is the one that *best* answers the question.

Tips for Mathematical Tests

- **Try to estimate the answer.**
  Before you solve a mathematical question, try to estimate the answer. For example, if you are asked to find 17.5% of a number, round off the amount to 15% and 20%, so you know the answer will fall between those two amounts. Then cross out the answer choices that do not fall within your estimate. Solve the problem and look at the choices to find the one that matches your solution.

- **Draw diagrams to help you think out problems.**
  Diagrams and pictures are especially helpful for math problems that involve shapes, lengths, distances, and sizes.

- **Rephrase word problems.**
  Restating word problems in your own words helps you understand the problem and its different parts. Then try to relate this word problem to others you have done. This will help you see similar solutions.

- **Be sure to show the answer in the correct mathematical form.**
  Even if your answer is correct, it will likely be marked wrong if it is in the wrong form, such as decimals instead of fractions. Reread the test question to make sure you are stating your answer in the correct form. Check to see if the simplest form is required. For example, you might have to write $\frac{1}{2}$ instead of $\frac{4}{8}$.

- **Show all your work.**
  Be sure to show all your work, because you can sometimes get partial credit for correct work even if you made a counting error.

- **Check your answers.**
  Even if you are sure that you got the correct answer, always try to make time to check your work. This can help you catch errors in counting, plus/minus signs, and logic.

- **Use common sense.**
  If an answer doesn't seem right even if you found a matching answer choice, trust your instincts. Recalculate the problem to see where the error occurred. Make sure that you are working the metric or standard (English) system, whatever form is required.

Tips for Taking Standardized Tests

Standardized tests are similar to classroom tests in many ways, but they have a few significant differences. These differences change the strategies you use.

- **Recognize the order of difficulty.**
  The test items on standardized tests are often arranged from easier to more difficult. As you work through the test, the questions will get more and more difficult. Therefore, you will have to budget your time differently. Spend less time on the first questions and more time on the last questions.

- **Be prepared not to know everything.**
  You can (and do!) study for a classroom test. As a result, you'll be able to ace the test because you know the material and test-taking strategies. This is not true with most standardized tests. You can prepare by learning the types of information you can expect, but you can't study the specific material because the content isn't known beforehand. As a result, there will most likely be questions you can't answer. Don't be upset; this is the way the test is designed.

- **Bring the correct supplies.**
  Always bring a calculator with you to the test, whether you think you will need it or not. It is better to have a calculator and not need it than to need it and not have one. Also bring at least three sharpened #2 pencils and a pen.

SUPER ESSAY TEST HINTS

Earning a high score on essay tests isn't difficult if you prepare, practice, and learn some test-taking strategies. Start by practicing your writing under pressure.

As you do when you study for short-answer tests, create your own essay test questions and write the answers. Look over the textbook, your notes, and any past tests you took to predict what topics the teacher will ask this time. Then answer your practice questions within the specific time you will be given on the test. This is especially helpful if you have trouble writing in a set time. Once you've prepared for the test, you'll feel more confident.

Following are some strategies to use as you take the test.

Read the Entire Test Before You Start to Write

Read *all* the directions *all* the way through before you begin to write anything. Reading all the directions first helps you understand the assignment and all its parts before you start to write. You don't want to find out halfway through the test that you have misunderstood the question or task.

If you have to write similar essay tests all the time, memorize the directions. This can save you valuable time you can apply to the writing itself.

> **T**
> **I**
> **P**
>
> **Are you nervous about essay tests? If so, relax! A minor case of the nerves can actually help you when you write an essay test because it keeps you alert and focused.**

Get the Guidelines

Go back over the instructions to get the essay's guidelines. Here's what you want to know before you choose your question and start to write:

- Audience: Who will be reading my writing? What do they expect from me?

- Purpose: Why am I writing? Below are the three main purposes tested in pressure-writing situations:
  - to convince someone that your opinion is correct
  - to convey information about a topic
  - to tell a story
- Length: How long should my essay be? Do I have to write a paragraph, three paragraphs, or even four paragraphs?
- Time: How long do I have to write? The amount of time I have determines how I plan and write.

Underline Key Words

After you read the essay question or questions and get the guidelines, underline any key words in the question to help you understand what you have to do. Writers under pressure often forget to answer an important part of a question. Underlining the key words in the question helps you safeguard against this problem. For example, if the question asks "Summarize the key events in the French Revolution," underline *summarize* and *French Revolution*.

Determine the Response

Now figure out what type of questions you are being asked. There are four main types of essay questions: *recall, analyze, evaluate,* and *synthesize*.

- **Recall Essay Questions**
  On these tests, your teacher wants to find out what facts you have learned. As a result, you must remember facts and summarize them in a logical essay. Here are some recall questions:

  Write an account of the American Revolution as if you were there.

  What can everyone do to conserve energy?

Trace how the continents were formed.

There are two methods of organization well suited to recall writing tests:

- Order of importance: Present the facts from most to least important.

- Chronological order: Present the information in time order.

How can you tell if the essay focuses on recall? Read the test closely to see if it's designed to find out if you've *read* the material or whether you've *extended* what you learned. If it's the first choice, then you're dealing with a recall essay. In that case, you should write an essay filled with facts, details, and examples.

- **Analyze Essay Questions**
With these essay questions, your teacher wants to find out how well you've made sense of what you've heard in class and read at home. When you *analyze*, you separate something into parts, examine each part, and show how they relate to the whole. This shows the teacher that you got the main idea.

Essay tests that ask you to analyze usually contain one or more of these key words:

analyze	assess	clarify
classify	describe	determine
examine	explain	explicate
explore	interpret	probe
review	show	support

Here are some analysis questions:

Analyze the causes of the American Revolution.

Explain what happens in the story "Charles," by Shirley Jackson.

Describe the causes and effects of the Industrial Revolution.

Show why it is important to recycle.

- **Evaluate Essay Questions**
Here's where the teacher asks you to make judgments by applying your beliefs to the topic. You back up your opinion with details and examples from your reading and notes.

Here are some essay questions that ask you to *evaluate*:

Pretend you were a Loyalist, a colonist who sided with the British during the American Revolution. Argue that the colonists should remain loyal to England and not rebel.

Imagine you could have any pet you wished. Select a pet and explain why you want to raise it.

Are computers being overemphasized in our schools? Argue yes or no.

If there were limited room on the last spacecraft to depart from a doomed Earth, someone would have to select the passengers. Among the characters you have met in the readings we have done this year, nominate two who you feel would qualify for consideration. Describe why each character deserves to be aboard the spacecraft.

- **Synthesize Essay Questions**
Synthesizing generally requires the most creativity because it includes all the other tasks — recall, analysis, and evaluation. To get a good grade on these tests, use the facts to analyze the question and reach a conclusion. You will be graded on your logic and original thinking. You can arrange your information this way:

- Open with your main idea. Give an overview of the point you'll be making.

- Support your point with details and examples.

- Reach a logical and intelligent conclusion.

Here are some essay questions that ask you to synthesize information:

Imagine that America lost the Revolutionary War. Describe what life would be like in America now.

While shopping with a friend and your younger sister, you see another shopper slip a small object into a shopping bag. What do you do and say?

Would you rather be popular with an entire group without forming a really close friendship, or have one very close friend but not be popular with the group? Explain your answer.

If you could choose any special power you wished, what would it be and why? How would you use this power?

T I P

Even before you get your essay back, think about your performance. What could you have done better? For example, did you use your time wisely? Did you find the best possible structure and present your points in a logical order? You might wish to try other strategies on your next essay test.

If you have a choice of essay questions, figure out which one you can answer the best. Choose the question you know the most about because you have studied that topic most completely.

Use the Writing Process

There are three main steps in the writing process:

- Planning
- Drafting
- Revising

Using the writing process on essay tests helps you approach the writing task logically. As a result, you'll be more likely to include all the important facts and examples in the correct order. You'll be more likely to avoid panic, too, since you're organized.

When you *plan* your essay, you . . .

- prewrite by listing ideas, making charts and diagrams, and asking yourself the 5W's and H (Who? What? When? Where? Why? and How?).
- choose which ideas to include and which ones to omit.
- arrange your ideas in a logical way. Use a web, map, or outline to help you see links between ideas.

When you *draft* your essay, you . . .

- write your first copy.

When you *revise* your essay, you . . .

- add facts that you need to make your point.
- cross out details that are off the topic.
- rearrange information so the essay is more logical and unified.
- use as much time as allowed.
- correct errors in spelling, punctuation, capitalization, grammar, and usage.
- write your final copy.

Here's how Angel used the writing process to write an essay on the topic "Describe how children can help preserve the environment." In this essay, Angel will synthesize what he recalls about the environment, how he has helped, and other things that people can do to help our world. Angel made this web to brainstorm ideas:

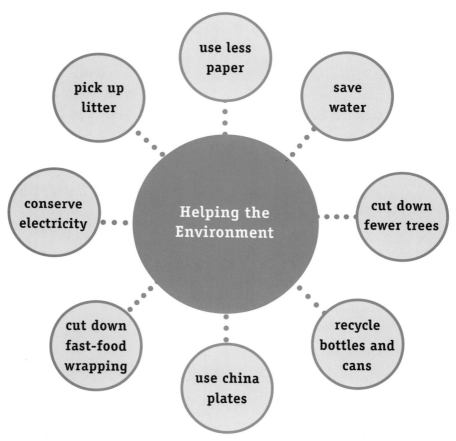

Here is Angel's first draft:

I am just a person. I am not the president, the governor, or the mayor. I will probably never be any of those people. I can do as much as they can do to help the environment.

I and you, and everyone in the world, can makes a diference in many ways. We can recycle bottles and cans we can use less paper by using china plates rather than paper plates This will help clean up the world. We can make fast-food chains not wrap their food in so many layers of paper. We eat fast food every Saturday when my parents are busy cleaning the house.

In the time it takes you too blink, do you know how many trees are cut down? How many elephants are slaughtered for their tusks and their meat left to rot? How much gasoline is wasted?

Planets like Earth aren't a dime a dozen. We all have two work together for a healthy environment. You can. I am just one person. I can make a difference.

Use Specific Details

As you learned in Section Two, details take the form of facts, examples, statistics, reasons, definitions, and descriptions. Use details to convince your reader that you know the subject. Details also make your writing vivid and specific. Look back at the details that Angel brainstormed to use in his essay.

This fine essay written by a sixth grader on a social studies test contains many details. They are underlined. The writer was asked to explain Hammurabi's laws.

Hammurabi was a Babylonian ruler who <u>created an empire,</u> <u>built the first libraries,</u> and <u>set up two types of written laws:</u> the <u>Laws of Retaliation</u> and the <u>Laws of Compensation.</u> These laws were very important because they were the <u>most complete set of laws at that time.</u>

The two sets of laws were very different. <u>Under the Laws of Retaliation, if someone did you harm, then you were allowed to treat them the same way.</u> For example, <u>if your neighbor killed your chickens, you were allowed to kill his chickens.</u> The same was true <u>if you harmed someone.</u>

The Laws of Compensation were different. According to these laws, <u>if someone stole something from you, they would be forced to pay a fine or go to jail.</u> As a result, the Laws of Compensation were <u>similar to some of today's</u>

laws. Today, if you commit a crime <u>such as</u> <u>driving while intoxicated, you would probably</u> <u>have to pay a fine or serve a jail sentence</u>. Clearly, the Laws of Retaliation were harsher than the Laws of Compensation.

Link Ideas with Connecting Words

Connect related ideas with linking words. These words and phrases tie your ideas together and create logic. The following chart shows some of the most useful connecting words. The relationship is listed on the left, the connecting words on the right.

SIGNAL	CONNECTING WORD	
Addition	also	in addition
	too	and
	besides	further
	next	then
	finally	moreover
Example	for example	for instance
	namely	specifically
Contrast	nevertheless	nonetheless
	yet	in contrast
	but	still
	however	on the other hand
Comparison	in comparison	similarly
	likewise	in the same way
Concession	naturally	granted
	certainly	to be sure
	of course	

SIGNAL	CONNECTING WORD	
Place	nearby	in the distance
	here	there
	at the side	next to
	adjacent	in the front
	in the back	
Result	due to this	so
	accordingly	consequently
	as a result	therefore
Summary	finally	in conclusion
	in summary	in brief
	as a result	hence
	on the whole	in short
Time Order	first	second
	third	fourth (etc.)
	next	subsequently
	immediately	later
	eventually	in the future
	currently	now
	during	meanwhile
	before	soon
	afterward	at length
	finally	then

Write Clearly, Concisely, and Carefully

The most successful essays always fulfill their purpose, address their audience, and have a logical organization. This is true whether the essay is written at home or during a test.

Winning essays are also neat. A good answer isn't good at all if it can't be read. Some teachers will take points off for sloppy work. Be sure to write or print neatly.

Below is Angel's final draft. Notice how he added the facts he needs to make his point, crossed out details that are off the topic, and rearranged information so his essay is more logical and unified. He also added connecting words and corrected all the errors in spelling, punctuation, capitalization, grammar, and usage. His essay achieves its purpose — to convince readers that children can help save the environment. It also addresses his audience (the teacher) and is organized logically, point by point.

Helping the Environment

I am just a person. I am not the president, the governor, or the mayor. I will probably never be any of those people. I can do as much as they can do to help the environment, however.

You and I, and everyone in the world, can make a difference. Just by picking up litter, saving water, and conserving electricity we can help clean up the world. We can also recycle bottles and cans. In addition, we can use less paper by using china plates rather than paper plates and insist that fast-food chains not wrap their food in so many layers of paper.

In the time it takes you to blink, do you know how many trees are cut down? How many elephants are slaughtered for their tusks and their meat left to rot? How much gasoline is wasted because people won't carpool to work and on chores?

Planets like Earth aren't a dime a dozen. We all have to work together for a healthy environment. I am just one person, but I can make a difference. You can, too.

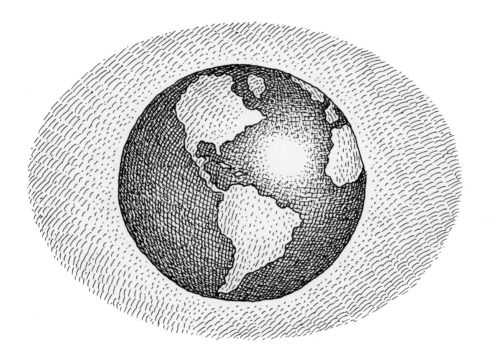

Use the Rubric

Many tests are evaluated according to a *rubric*. A rubric shows what you must include in your essay to earn a high score. If your teacher gives the class a rubric, study it. See what you must include in your essay. Keep the rubric in mind as you write.

Here is a general rubric. You can use it for any writing you do.

FOURTH/FIFTH GRADE WRITING RUBRIC

4

Focus	Always stays on topic, establishes and maintains a clear purpose
Content	Abundant information and details specific to topic
Organization	Strong introduction and conclusion, appropriate paragraphing, logical sequencing, consistent transitions between sentences
Style	Precise language, superior word choice, clear voice, originality of language; variety of sentence structures, types, and lengths
Conventions	Very few mechanical and usage errors (spelling, grammar, capitalization, complete sentences, punctuation)

3

Focus	Mostly stays on topic, establishes and maintains clear purpose
Content	Comprehensive information and details to topic
Organization	Logical transitions made between most sentences and between paragraphs; introduction and conclusion evident
Style	Effective word choice, some attempt at voice, originality of language; some variety of sentence structures, types, and lengths
Conventions	Some mechanical and use errors (spelling, grammar, capitalization, complete sentences, punctuation)

2

Focus	Usually stays on topic, may not have a clear message or purpose
Content	Offers information and details specific to topic; some information may be unrelated to topic or inaccurate
Organization	Inconsistent use of introduction and conclusion, sequencing, use of paragraphs, and transition words and sentences
Style	Limited originality in word choice and sentence variety, occasional voice
Conventions	Many mechanical, spelling, and usage errors (spelling, grammar, capitalization, complete sentences, punctuation)

1

Focus	Rarely stays on topic, a clear purpose not established
Content	Little information and details specific to topic
Organization	No transitions are made between sentence and between paragraphs; introduction and conclusion not evident
Style	Poor word choice, limited sentence variety, no voice
Conventions	Serious mechanical and usage errors (spelling, grammar, capitalization, complete sentences, punctuation)

Adapted from rubric provided by the Centennial School District in Warminster, PA.

T
I
P

Be sure to proofread. No one expects a *perfect* paper in a pressure-writing situation, but sloppy errors undercut your thinking and can sink even the best papers.

Budget Your Time

You learned in Section Four how much time you can spend planning, drafting, and revising to complete your essay in the time allowed. As you write, try not to get bogged down in rough patches. If you do get stuck, leave some spaces and keep writing. With pressure-writing situations, time is key.

Pace yourself by taking a deep breath every 10 to 15 minutes, putting down your pen for a moment, and stretching. You want to work at a slow, steady pace. Slow and steady wins the race!

Answer the Specific Question

Make sure that your essay really answers the question fully and completely. Have you addressed all the key points? Have you shown that you fully understand the topic?

When you're writing under pressure, it's tempting to remake the topic into something you feel more comfortable answering. Be sure you're answering the question you have been asked, not one you misread or made up.

And as you have already learned, if you have time left over, don't waste it.

> **T I P**
>
> **If you run out of time before you can finish writing your essay, jot down what you were going to say in a few complete sentences. Your teacher may be able to give you some extra credit even though you didn't finish writing the entire essay.**

Below is a brief essay written by a sixth grader. The essay was part of a science test. The student was asked to tell about lightning. The essay earned an "A" because it stays on the topic (lightning), uses language and details appropriate for the reader (the teacher), and has a clear method of organization.

A Bolt from the Blue

Have you ever heard the famous old saying "Lightning never strikes twice in the same place"? This old saying is often exposed as false and probably not too many educated people believe it. But many people are not aware of the real facts behind lightning. Not only does lightning often strike twice in the same place, but it is more likely to do so. Why is this so? Lightning is an electric current. As with all electric currents or discharges, lightning will follow the path of least resistance. This means that it will take the route that is easiest for it to travel on. It is hard for lightning to travel through the air. As a result, almost anything else that helps to bridge the gap between the ground and a cloud — a high tree, a building (especially one with a metal framework), a tall hill — will attract the lightning. That's why lightning is more likely to strike twice in the same place.

Use a Checklist

Many writers find it helpful to use a checklist when they have to write under pressure. Use the following checklist to get you started.

PRESSURE-WRITING CHECKLIST

Preparation

_____ Did I study by reviewing my textbook and notes?

_____ Did I get enough sleep?

_____ Have I eaten?

_____ Am I in the right place taking the correct test?

Planning

_____ Have I read the directions? Do I understand the task?

_____ Did I read the entire test before I started to write?

_____ Do I understand the guidelines? (audience, purpose, length, time)

_____ Do I understand the question? Have I found the key words?

_____ Do I understand the response? (recall, analyze, evaluate, synthesize)

_____ If I have a choice, have I selected the question I can answer most fully?

_____ Have I made a simple outline?

_____ Have I read the rubric?

Writing

_____ As I write, am I following the writing process?

_____ Have I budgeted my time well?

_____ Am I answering the specific question I have been asked?

_____ Did I include details and facts?

_____ Do I link ideas with connecting words?

_____ Are my facts correct?

Revising

_____ Have I included all the facts I need to make my point?

_____ Have I crossed out details that are off the topic?

_____ Have I arranged my facts in a logical way?

_____ Have I corrected all errors in spelling?

_____ Have I corrected all errors in punctuation?

_____ Have I corrected all errors in capitalization?

_____ Have I corrected all errors in grammar?

_____ Have I corrected all errors in usage (their/there/there, etc.)?

_____ Have I used all my time?

_____ Have I labeled every part of my response with my name and other necessary information?

_____ Did I hand in everything required, such as scrap paper and the test booklet as well as the finished essay?

P.S.

Test taking and studying are skills that can be learned. It takes time and effort to be a super test taker, but your investment will pay off now and in the future. You'll do better in school today and you'll have the tools you need to shape the future you want — and deserve.

Take a minute to congratulate yourself. You've set goals for yourself and planned ways to make them come true. Now you've started getting organized and taking responsibility for your own learning. Perhaps you've already gotten a study buddy and set up your study center. You've learned how to take good notes and make the most of your time.

After finishing this book, you know some powerful techniques for reading more effectively, too. You prepare carefully for a test by organizing and reviewing your notes and the textbook. You've gone over ways to calm test jitters. You know how to prepare, budget your time, and get a test strategy for short-answer and essay tests. After a test, you evaluate what you did right and what you can do better so you can study even smarter next time.

Anything worth doing requires hard work. Becoming a super student is no exception. Some of the world's most successful people were struggling students who learned how to read, study, and take tests more effectively. Now you, too, have the keys to the kingdom of success.